SADCC: ENERGY AND DEVELOPMENT TO THE YEAR 2000

Edited by
Jorge Tavares de Carvalho Simoes

Published by
SADCC ENERGY SECTOR

in collaboration with

THE BEIJER INSTITUTE
The Royal Swedish
Academy of Sciences
Stockholm, Sweden

THE SCANDINAVIAN INSTITUTE
OF AFRICAN STUDIES
Uppsala, Sweden

The series "Energy, Environment and Development in Africa" is published jointly by the Beijer Institute and the Scandinavian Institute of African Studies with financial support from the Swedish
International Development Authority (SIDA). This book   together
with a series of companion volumes reports on a study of Energy and
Development in the SADCC countries, jointly undertaken by the SADCC
Energy Sector and the various member states of SADCC in collaboration
with the Beijer Institute.

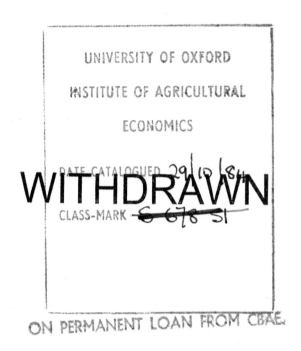
ISSN 0281-8515
ISBN 91-7106-227-0

© the Beijer Institute and the Scandinavian Institute of
   African Studies 1984

Printed in Sweden by
Bohusläningens AB, Uddevalla 1984

FOREWORD

Energy is critical for development, but successful development requires careful planning. This planning must take into account the energy requirements that are needed to power the development process. It is, therefore, a pleasure to present this initial contribution aimed at strengthening energy planning capability in the SADCC region.

The ~~present~~ volume is the first of four devoted to energy in the Southern African Development Coordination Conference (SADCC) Region. It contains the summarized results of the Regional Energy Planning Seminar run by the member-states of SADCC, coordinated by the People's Republic of Angola and hosted by the Republic of Zimbabwe, in December 1982. Member countries of SADCC initially suggested the need for such a Seminar at the United Nations Conference on New and Renewable Sources of Energy (Nairobi, 1981). Plans for the Seminar were completed in May, 1982, and at SADCC's request the necessary fieldwork required to augment the available energy data in the Region was carried out by the Beijer Institute team between June and October 1982. As a result, background documents were prepared for the Seminar. Two further volumes containing this background material, scheduled to appear later in this series, are devoted to individual country case studies of energy and development in the nine member states. A final background volume outlines an analysis of industrial development in the SADCC region.

The regional energy picture is positive. There are abundant supplies of commercial energy resources within the region. The challenge facing SADCC members is to devise the technical, economic, institutional and political arrangements that will enable these resources to be effectively utilized in the development of the Region. This is especially important because, without modern development, the continued reliance on traditional wood - and other biomass-fuels will result in environmental degradation.

What is clearly required is the development of an overall energy strategy that considers both modern and traditional fuel sources and ties these resources to specific end-uses. This approach could provide accurate estimates of future demand in all energy sectors so that investments in supply can be made at the right level of response to meet these future needs. This and the subsequent volumes go some way towards establishing such a process.

The work of the Beijer team members would not have been possible, if support had not so readily been given by government officials in the Region. In particular, I would like to thank the Minister for Energy and Petroleum of the People's Republic of Angola, the Hon. Pedro de Castro dos Santos Van-Dunem, and the Minister for Industry and Energy of the Republic of Zimbabwe, The Hon. Simba Makoni, M.P. for supporting these efforts. It is a pleasure to acknowledge the support at the Seminar of Secretary General F. Arthur Blumeris of the SADCC Secretariat. Our special gratitude and sincere thanks go to Professor Gordon Goodman, the Director of the Beijer Institute, to Professor Phil O'Keefe, Dr Barry Munslow and to other members of the Beijer team including Dr Paul Raskin of the Energy Systems Research Group for producing the excellent factual and analytical background material for the Seminar, for their superb feat of technical organisation that lay behind the smooth running of the Seminar, and for all their work on the contents of this Volume, particularly the Summary Overview (pp. 5 -83). I am also pleased to acknowledge the financial assistance of the Swedish International Development Authority (SIDA) which has made the original work and its present publication possible. In particular I should like to thank Mr Lars Berggren of SIDA's Industrial Division, who attended the Seminar, for his interest in the project. Finally I would like to thank Molly Akerlund of the Beijer Institute Secretariat, Tim Sheehy and Cathy Attlee of the SADCC Secretariat for providing their usual wise advice and enthusiastic support throughout the preparatory and final stages of the Seminar and June Summers for her rapid production of the typescript comprising this Volume. It is with the conviction that the material in these volumes will prove useful also in a much wider context, in addition to the original audience at the Harare Seminar, that we are undertaking its publication. However we are all very conscious of the fact that it represents only a small contribution to what must be a continuing effort to find solutions to the problems of planning for energy provision in the SADCC Region.

Jorge Tavares de Carvalho Simoes   October, 1983
Regional Coordinator
SADCC Energy Sector

INTRODUCTION.

This volume is the product of the first regional energy seminar held within the context of the Southern African Development Coordinating Coference programme. The meeting was convened in Harare (29 November to 3 December, 1982) and was hosted by the Government of the Republic of Zimbabwe and chaired by the People's Republic of Angola, the country responsible for energy coordination in SADCC. It provides the first comprehensive overview of the regional energy situation and projections of energy demand and supply to the year 2000.

The research was carried out and completed in 1982. The study involved a number of components. Firstly, detailed field research was carried out in each of the SADCC member states: Angola, Botswana, Lesotho, Malawi, Mozambique, Swaziland, Tanzania, Zambia and Zimbabwe. Nine in-depth country profiles were produced and these form the basis for separate and subsequent volumes. As an important cross-checking mechanism and to produce a fuller and more complete analysis, sectoral studies were also undertaken on industry, transport, demography and woodfuel. The industry study was highly detailed and had an enormous scope; this is being produced as a subsequent volume in its own right. Completed manuscripts on transport and woodfuel are obtainable from the Beijer Institute. Copies of all original materials are obtainable from the Beijer Institute, The Royal Swedish Academy of Sciences.

The present volume provides a summary overview of these findings in a concise format, picking out the dominant themes in the regional energy picture. On the demand side, the national energy accounts are examined to detail the current and future energy consumption. On the supply side, each of the major fuel sources is discussed, including biomass, and regional self-sufficency of commercial fuels.The summary document then considers policy issues. These include,

- Regional and national energy planning
- Regional oil coordination
- Integrated grid systems
- Expanded coal utilisation
- Traditional energy sources
- Conservation.

The possibilities for further action are considered including the planning tasks, national energy assessment, regional energy assessment, regional energy projects, regional energy centres and planning procedures.

Following the overview document are the conclusions emanating from the nine member governments participating in the seminar suggesting positive ways forward for further activity in regional energy coordination.

The member states of SADCC have also produced statements on their government's energy policies. These provide information on the institutional framework within which policies are formulated and implemented. They provide an assessment of energy needs and resources, examine future trends and note the shortfalls in energy data where these occur. In addition, they examine existing and projected energy development programmes.

Finally, the volume includes the two important speeches made at the opening and close of the energy seminar. The first was made by Simba Makoni, Minister of Industry and Energy Development of the Republic of Zimbabwe, and the second by Pedro van-Dunem, Minister of Energy and Petroleum of the People's Republic of Angola.

Energy Equivalents

To Convert From	into	Mtoe	Mboe	Mtce	Bm^3 Gas	TWh	PJ
Million tonnes oil equivalent (Mtoe)		1	7.33	1.55	1.15	12.60	44.93
Million barrels oil equivalent (Mboe)		0.136	1	0.21	0.156	1.71	6.17
Million tonnes coal equivalent (Mtce)		0.65	4.74	1	0.74	8.14	29.31
Million (10^9) cubic metres natural gas (Bm^3 gas)		0.87	6.41	1.34	1	10.93	39.26
Tera watt hours (10^{12} watt hours: TWh)		0.079	0.58	0.12	0.091	1	3.6
Peta joule (10^{15} joule: PJ)		0.022	0.16	0.034	0.025	0.28	1
Wood equivalents Mill tonnes wood equivalent (Mtwe)		0.356	2.61	0.55	0.41	4.49	16.00

e.g. 1 million barrels oil (mboe) = 0.136 million tonnes oil (Mtoe)

Power Equivalents

To Convert From	into	Mtoe/yr	Mbd	Mtce/yr	GWth	PJ/yr
Mtoe/year (Mtoe/yr)		1	0.02	1.55	1.43	45
Mb/day (Mbd)		50	1	77	71	2235
Mtce/year (Mtce/yr)		0.65	0.013	1	0.92	29
Giga watt (10 watt) thermal (GW_{th})		0.70	0.014	1.09	1	32
PJ/year (PJ/yr)		0.02	4.5×10^{-4}	0.034	0.031	1

Energy Content Of Selected Fuels

Fuel	Energy Content*
Wood**	16.0 GJ/tonne
Charcoal	33.1 GJ/tonne
Crop Residue**	13.9 GJ/tonne
Dung**	12.8 GJ/tonne
Bottled Gas	.0452 GJ/KG
Kerosene	.0391 GJ/litre
Gasoline	.0344 GJ/litre
Diesel	.0387 GJ/litre
Residual Oil	.0390 GJ/litre
Jet Turbo	.0351 GJ/litre
Crude Oil	6.17 GJ/barrel

* Expressed in 10^9 joules (GJ) per physical unit.
** Biomass figures assumed air-dried to 15% moisture content. Actual values vary with species. Average wood volume to weight conversion: 1.4 M^3 = tonne.

SADCC: ENERGY AND DEVELOPMENT TO THE YEAR 2000

TABLE OF CONTENTS

LIST OF TABLES

SPEECH BY THE MINISTER OF INDUSTRY AND ENERGY DEVELOPMENT
OF THE REPUBLIC OF ZIMBABWE AT THE OFFICIAL
OPENING OF THE SADCC ENERGY SEMINAR.

Harare, 29th November 1982.

It is a great pleasure for me personally, my Ministry, and the Government of the Republic of Zimbabwe to welcome all our guests to Zimbabwe. I particularly wish to welcome you, Cde. Blumeris, Executive Secretary of SADCC and thank you for finding time to be with us during this week. To you our cooperants from the Beijer Institute and the Swedish International Development Agency (SIDA),I extend a very warm welcome. I sincerely hope that you will find the arrangements satisfactory and wish you a pleasant stay in Zimbabwe.

We are all gathered here this week to attend the first ever SADCC Energy Sectoral Seminar. The Beijer Institute first proposed, in early 1981, to sponsor a seminar for Zimbabwean energy planners and experts. But after full consultations with our sister partners in SADCC, it was agreed that this become a regional energy seminar in the context of SADCC energy sector programme development. I wish to register Zimbabwe's gratitude and appreciation to our SADCC partners for having chosen our country as the venue for this important occasion.

The availability of energy of various forms in adequate quantities and at affordable prices is increasingly becoming a decisive factor in development. Economic development, particularly industrialisation, after the Second World War was fuelled by cheap, apparently inexhaustible oil and electrical power. In recent years, the balance between supply and demand of energy has been greatly disturbed; and yet energy, in its different forms, is a basic prerequisite for normal societal functioning, irrespective of the state of organisation or development of the society in question.

Our seminar is convened to address the questions of energy planning and management as part of the strategy for regional cooperation. Some of the specific areas of concern to us during this seminar are:

- To assess the energy supply and demand position in our region:

- To identify and quantify the various forms of energy available in the region, as well as to determine the extent of utilisation or under-utilisation of each form:

- To consider the opportunities for and constraints on future energy development, including assessments of human resource, technical and financial requirements:

- To formulate the planning requirements for the enhancement of SADCC energy cooperation.

Our region is endowed with substantial and varied energy resources. We, collectively, have installed capacity for power generation which is double our peak demand requirements. Thus, the region as a whole has a massive power surplus. Within the region, hydro-electric power generation accounts for over 60 per cent of total power output, a small part is produced by oil-powered generators and the balance is from coal-fired stations. Some of our member states engage in trade in power both amongst themselves as well as with outsiders. Thus, although the region as a whole has surplus power, there is no overall regional self-sufficiency.

This situation is a colonial legacy for which none of us is responsible. But, this situation is, in my view, one of the most rational justifications for SADCC. For it is urgently imperative that we take steps to speedily eliminate this irony.

But it is even more urgent that as we individually or collectively plan for our future, we take into full account the available capacities before we install new ones. To this extent, some of the proposed or potential projects for interconnecting national power grids are most desirable. It is also important that in planning for future power facilities, careful site selection be undertaken to facilitate regional inter-connection and integration. The formulation of least-cost, longterm regional power development plans will facilitate the eradication of the present contradictions of surpluses in some countries and deficiencies in others which characterise our present situation.

Petroleum fuels account for a substantial portion of our energy consumption. But all of our countries, except one, have no petroleum deposits. Thus, the region as a whole depends on imported oil and or oil products. It is, however, noteworthy, that the proven and exploitable oil reserves in the one member state, are capable of meeting the needs of the whole SADCC region. I am sure that you will all join me in hoping that the indications of possible oil finds in other member states of SADCC will be confirmed. In addition to the availability, within the region, of adequate oil reserves, it is common knowledge that we have adequate, if not surplus, refining capacity. This leads to the situation where, in some member states, refineries are either idle or operating well below capacity, while other member states are importing refined products. It is, therefore, important that we work out a mechanism that enables us to utilise the available resources and facilities to the collective and mutual benefit of all the member states. In this regard, I am gratified that SADCC Ministers of Energy decided to sponsor, for donor funding, a project study on the best ways of meeting the region's petroleum requirements primarily from resources already within the region. It is my fervent hope that this project will be speedily implemented.

Our region is also well-endowed with coal deposits. Seven of our nine member states have established coal resources, and mining is underway in six of them. It is estimated that our proven coal reserves amount to about 12 billion tonnes and consumption at present averages about four million tonnes annually. There is, therefore, ample scope for greater and diversified utilisation of coal than at present.

Whereas the foregoing indicates that this region is capable of meeting its requirements of commercial energy, it provides no comfort for the vast majority of our people who live in the rural areas. These are the worst victims of racist colonialism and, therefore, the primary target of our national as well as cooperative regional development efforts. The search for energy to meet the modest requirements of our rural population has become a burdensome and agonising chore paralleled, if not marginally excelled, only by the search for food.

The spectacle of our women-folk travelling long distances to collect small bundles of firewood has become a common feature of our rural life. All of our countries are faced with serious problems of forest denudation which poses grave dangers to our environment. This area presents the greatest challenge for our countries; for its effects will be felt not only in the energy field but in many other areas. It is regrettable that planners tend to under rate, if not actually ignore, the importance of this commodity.

The general area of New and Renewable Sources of Energy (NRSE) holds meaningful prospects for meeting some of our energy requirements.

The climatic conditions of our region render viable the harnessing of the sun, wind and other resources for energy supplies. But, much as we recognise, and indeed, emphasize the potential role of NRSE in our economies, I must sound a word of caution. At the international level, there is a growing tendency to promote NRSE as the solution to Third World energy problems; whilst at national levels the tendency is to offer NRSE as a solution to rural energy problems. In other words NRSE become the energy of the poor whilst the established commercial energies are channelled to assuage the insatiable appetites of the rich. In order to avoid the consolidation and perpetuation of present energy imbalances, all forms of energy must be equitably distributed to all sectors of the economy and the society.

Cde. Chairman, I have attempted, in the foregoing, to expose the characteristic features of the energy sector in our region and the problems attendant thereto. I have not attempted to offer, let alone prescribe, solutions to those problems. I would urge that this seminar be a forum for seeking down-to-earth practical solutions to problems, rather than becoming a forum for high-sounding academic or political pontifications. Our people need energy now, not tomorrow; and we must pave the way for meeting that need.

In conclusion, Cde. Chairman, I would like to express our gratitude,i.e. SADCC's gratitude, to the Beijer Institute and the Swedish International Development Agency for sponsoring and funding this seminar. Our gratitude also goes to the SADCC secretariat for its assistance in the practical arrangements for this gathering. We are also grateful to the various experts, both national and international who worked so hard to produce a wealth of background documentation, without which our task here would be well nigh impossible.

Finally, it gives me great pleasure to declare open this SADCC Energy Seminar, and I wish us success in our deliberations.

Thank you.

1. INTRODUCTION

This document provides a background summary of the energy situation in each of the nine countries comprising the Southern African Development Coordination Conference (SADCC), and identifies opportunities for cooperative regional energy planning. The objective is to contribute to the evolving SADCC discussions on energy cooperation by providing a summary of the current supply and demand picture and a glimpse of the long-range patterns, and by raising issues for ongoing discussion and action.

1.A SADCC

SADCC was formally founded at a Summit Conference in Lusaka in April, 1980. The member countries are:

   The People's Republic of Angola;
   The Republic of Botswana;
   The Kingdom of Lesotho;
   The Republic of Malawi;
   The People's Republic of Mozambique;
   The Kingdom of Swaziland;
   The United Republic of Tanzania;
   The Republic of Zambia;
   The Republic of Zimbabwe.

The founding declaration signed in Lusaka, entitled Southern Africa: Toward Economic Liberation, gives four objectives for SADCC:

   (a) Reduction of economic dependence, particularly, but not only, on the Republic of South Africa;

   (b) The forging of links to create a genuine and equitable regional integration;

   (c) The mobilisation of resources to promote the implementation of national, interstate and regional policies;

   (d) Concerted action to secure international co-operation within the framework of a strategy for economic liberation.

In pursuit of these goals, SADCC has established an institutional framework which includes:

   (a) A Summit Meeting of the Heads of State and/or Government of the Member States meeting annually and chaired by one of them - Botswana for 1981-84;

(b) A Council of Ministers to supervise the programme of
     SADCC, also meeting at least annually and presided over
     by a Chairman and Vice-Chairman elected from among their
     number - Botswana and Zimbabwe for 1981;

(c) A Standing Committee of Officials to service the Council
     of Ministers, with subcommittee (e.g. with respect to
     the veterinary, manpower and industrial coordination
     sectors) meeting regularly with the States holding
     delegated responsibility for the sector and reporting
     back to the Standing Committee of Officials;

(d) Sectoral Commissions established by the Summit through
     interstate Convention to cover programmes in high
     priority functional programme areas, of which the first
     is the Southern Africa Transport and Communications
     Commission (SATCC), based in Maputo;

(e) A Secretariat headed by an Executive Secretary to
     service the SADCC institutions and coordinate SADCC
     programme implementation, to come into operation in July
     1982 based in Gaborone, with a Zimbabwean as the first
     Executive Secretary.

(Southern African Development Coordination:
From Dependence and Poverty Toward Economic Liberation, SADCC,
Blantyre 1981)

A number of programme areas have now been created, with
coordination responsibility in each area delegated to a member
country (e.g. Transport and Communication to Mozambique, Food
Security to Zimbabwe, Industrial Development to Tanzania,
Development Fund to Zambia, Manpower Development to Swaziland,
Crop Research to Botswana).

1.B Project Background

The government of Angola is the SADCC coordinating country for
Energy Development and Conservation. In April, 1982, plans for a
SADCC Energy Seminar to be held November 29 through December 3,
1982, were finalized. The seminar, entitled Energy Redevelopment
in Southern Africa: Opportunities and Constraints, was to be
convened by Angola and hosted by Zimbabwe.

It was agreed that the Terms of Reference for the meeting would
be:

(a) To assess the national energy budgets of the SADCC
     Member Countries and project these budgets to the year
     2000.

(b) To place emphasis on both the demand and supply of traditional and commercial energy sources.

(c) To consider the opportunities and constraints of current energy development.

(d) To consider issues of human resources and technical development.

(e) To evaluate the industrial demand for commercial energy.

(f) To review all sectoral energy requirements, across SADCC countries, to the year 2000.

(g) To formulate planning requirements that enhance SADCC energy integration.

The Beijer Institute was commissioned to:

(1) Provide overall energy accounts for SADCC;

(2) Build those accounts on national energy reports;

(3) Provide a detailed analysis of the energy requirements of future industrial development;

(4) Solicit from the member states a policy statement about future energy directions;

(5) Prepare a synthesis document on SADCC energy planning;

(6) Make this material available for a SADCC energy meeting convened in Harare in November, 1982.

This report constitutes the synthesis document (Item 5).

Nine country experts were assigned to complete technical background papers on the national energy balances. Table 1 identifies the lead author for each country paper.

These papers were used as resource materials for developing the overall SADCC energy balances which are presented in this report. In addition, back-ground material was commissioned on the allied areas of transport (Colin Stoneman) and forestry (Barry Van Gelder). A major study was undertaken of industrial development and future energy requirements (Richard Peet). Finally, a review of the demographic conditions of the SADCC member countries was undertaken to enable the team to derive projections of future energy use to the year 2000 (Nancy Folbre).

TABLE 1

Lead Authors Of Background Documents

Country	Lead Author
Angola	Bhagavan
Botswana	Wisner
Lesotho	Frolich
Malawi	Scobey
Mozambique	Munslow
Swaziland	Munslow
Tanzania	Openshaw
Zambia	Susman
Zimbabwe	Hosier

The system employed to generate these national energy accounts is the LEAP energy accounting system. The system was developed for specific use in developing countries by the Energy Systems Research Group for the Beijer Institute. The accounting system balances demand and supply in the base year. Thereafter, a business-as-usual or Base Case scenario is presented against which a variety of policy interventions and specific projects could be tested. In June of 1982, the Energy Systems Research Group produced a first approximate set of energy balances for SADCC, using existing U.N. data and supplementary sources. These estimates were then revised after the field reports were produced.

The actual and projected energy use and supply figures contained in this volume reflect the project team's best current estimates based on the available data, identifiable trends, and energy sector plans. The analysis provides an overview of evolving national energy flow patterns, and a basis for the initial indentification of the major opportunities and issues for the ongoing energy coordination agenda.

In addition to the technical papers on each country, the relevant authorities in each of the SADCC member countries completed papers on their own respective energy policy. These papers are included in this volume and they were used to inform the current discussion. In passing, we would wish to note the complexity of institutional structures holding responsibility for energy within each member state.

1.C Report Plan

The body of the report begins with a discussion of energy demand in Section 2. The current situation is described for each country and for the region as a whole. Patterns across SADCC and specific country variations are discussed. The results of detailed projections to the year 2000 are then presented and long-term patterns identified. In Section 3, the energy resource side is described and regional energy supply/demand balances for major fuels are discussed.

Based on these results, a set of energy policy issues and broad strategic energy planning options are discussed in Section 4. Finally, Section 5 is devoted to identifying some options for enhanced institutional cooperation on energy planning and suggesting possibilities for further action.

Additionally, detailed country-specific information is presented in the form of computer output tables in the Annex. Since the reader may wish to refer to the material presented in the Annex at various times, either during or after reading the main body of this report, a basic description of the energy account tables is given in Section 2.

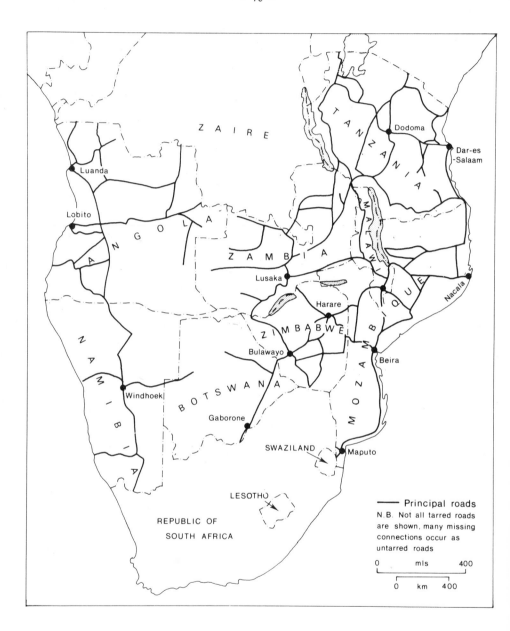

2. ENERGY DEMAND

In this section, estimates of current and projected end-use energy requirements are reported. The objective in developing these estimates is to give a systematic presentation of the main contours of the national energy pictures and thereby provide an initial quantitative basis for policy discussions.

The accuracy of the results and the level of detail are constrained by limitations on the existing energy-use data base (summarized in the country reports prepared by the project team). To varying extents, each country could benefit from improved, more detailed and centralized energy information management procedures. This is particularly the case with respect to data on the uses and sources of traditional fuels (fuelwood and agricultural residues) where, at best, crude estimates are available and, at worst, typical values from related studies must be employed. Nevertheless, the energy accounts do provide a sufficiently clear picture of the evolving energy situation in each country for this initial stage of the energy policy process. That picture could be sharpened at appropriate junctures in the national and regional planning contexts.

2.A National Energy Accounts

The energy requirement analysis has been performed by use of a computer-based energy assessment tool - the LDC Energy Alternatives Planning (LEAP) System. This allows for the systematic processing of data and for the development of current energy flow patterns and long-range demand forecasts.* The project effort has generated a prodigious amount of information on energy use patterns. That information has been distilled and summarized in the Annex at the back of this report.

The Annex consists of nine computer output tables for each of the SADCC member countries. These are grouped for each country in the order shown in Table 2.

---

* LEAP has been used primarily as an energy accounting tool in this exercise. In detailed planning efforts, other of its modules (demographic, agricultural, cost/benefit, biomass resources) are useful in generating scenarios and identifying and evaluating strategic options. These applications were beyond the scope of the current effort.

TABLE 2

Sequence Of Output Tables In Annex Report For Each Country

Output Table Name

---

1. 1980 Energy Balance
2. 1980 Detailed Consumption
3. 1990 Energy Balance
4. 1990 Detailed Consumption
5. Forecast National Consumption
6. Forecast Sectoral Consumption
7. Electrical Generation Summary
8. Petroleum Sources and Uses
9. Requirements in Physical Units

The first output table, the 1980 Energy Balance, traces the energy flows from primary resource requirements (e.g., crude oil, imported petroleum products, fuelwood), through energy conversion processes (e.g., electric generation, charcoal kilns, petroleum refinery), to aggregate final consumption by energy users. It takes account of conversion and other losses. This structure is shown schematically in Figure 1.

The second output table in the Annex sequence is the 1980 Detailed Consumption. The aggregate final consumption of fuels reported in the 1980 Energy Balance is composed of the consumptions of a variety of ultimate uses ("end-uses") across the economic sectors that comprise the national economy. The breakdown into selected sectors, subsectors, and end-uses is the subject of the 1980 Detailed Consumption table.

With sufficient information, it is possible to develop considerable detail on energy consumption by sector (e.g., household, industry), subsector (e.g., income group, product category), end-use (e.g., cooking, process heat), and device (e.g., stove type, process design). While such detail can be quite useful in national energy planning (we return to this issue in Section 5), the available information base supported only the limited disaggregation shown in Table 3, below. The fuel consumption results are most reliable for the commercial fuels at the sectoral levels Both subsectoral breakdowns and traditional fuel estimates are more speculative at this time.

The third and fourth output tables, appearing in the Annex and listed in Table 2 above, give the projected Energy Balance and Detailed Consumption, respectively, for 1990. The fifth displays

- 13 -

FIGURE 1.

SCHEMA OF ENERGY FLOWS

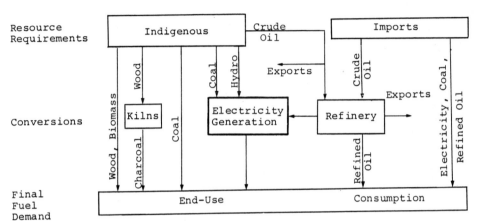

TABLE 3

DEMAND	CATEGORIES	EMPLOYED
Sector	Subsector/End-Use*	
Urban Household	Cooking Lighting Other	
Rural Household	Cooking Other	
Agriculture	Large Small	
Industry	Large Urban Informal Rural Cottage Construction Rural Poles	
Commercial/Institutional	All	
Transportation	Road (private, public) Rail (passenger, freight) Air Sea	

* These in turn are broken down by the fuel types utilized at the end-use.

the forecast of national consumption for each major fuel to the year 2000, while the sixth provides the fuel forecast by demand sector.

The seventh output table reports the projections of the electric generation system for each country. Anticipated capacity and output for each type of generating facility is shown, along with peak demand, system reserve margin (capacity in excess of peak demand), and electrical energy requirements. The eighth output table projects the sources and uses of petroleum, including refinery output, import requirements, and export levels. Finally, the ninth output table restates the national energy requirement in physical units rather than the energy units (petajoules) used in the other tables.

The reader interested in the detailed findings is referred to the annex compilations and the individual country reports. The subsections below are restricted to a summary of the results.

2.B The Current Picture

Before briefly reviewing the structure of energy demand for each member country, we shall consider the SADCC region as a whole. The SADCC countries had a joint population of 57.5 million in 1980, and an average gross national product of about US $380 per capita. The total 1980 final consumption of energy* was 1456 PJ or about 25 GJ (25×10^9 joules) per capita. This converts to about 850 kg coal equivalent (KgCe) per capita. Of this total, 306 PJ (180 KgCe per capita) or 21 per cent is consumed as so-called "commercial fuels", primarily electricity, coal, and petroleum products.** Fully 79 per cent of final consumption is derived from traditional fuels - biomass in the form of fuelwood, charcoal, and crop and animal residue. Not surprisingly, given its rough global correlation with per capita economic output, the per capita commercial fuel consumption in the SADCC region is relatively small. At the other extreme, by contrast, the per capita final energy consumption for Sweden and the U.S. are about 4500 and 9000 KgCe, respectively.

---

* Final consumption, it may be recalled, includes fuels utilized at the end-use. It does not include energy losses in distribution or in conversion to final fuel forms (e.g., electrical generation, charcoal production, petroleum refining).

** Animate forms of power (animal and human) are not included in the energy accounting in this report.

TABLE 4

1980 FINAL ENERGY CONSUMPTION (PJ) [1]
AND
AVERAGE ANNUAL GROWTH RATE 1980-2000 (%/Year)

| Country | Grand Total | Commercial Fuels [2] | | | | Traditional Fuels |
		Total	Electricity	Coal	Petroleum	
Angola						
PJ*	105.5	23.8	2.3	0.0	21.6	81.6
%/Year*	2.6	4.3	6.3	0.0	4.1	2.0
Botswana						
PJ	22.1	9.7	1.7	3.7	4.4	12.4
%/Year	3.3	4.0	4.3	3.6	4.1	2.8
Lesotho						
PJ	24.2	5.2	0.3	1.9	2.9	19.0
%/Year	2.4	4.2	6.4	5.1	3.2	1.8
Malawi						
PJ	165.2	9.4	1.3	1.4	6.7	155.8
%/Year	1.8	3.8	5.9	3.2	3.4	1.7
Mozambique						
PJ	281.7	30.6	2.5	5.8	22.3	251.1
%/Year	2.6	3.9	7.2	3.0	3.7	2.4
Swaziland						
PJ	24.0	9.6	1.6	3.3	4.7	14.4
%/Year	3.5	3.9	4.4	4.7	2.9	3.2
Tanzania						
PJ	438.9	37.5	2.3	0.2	35.0	401.4
%/Year	3.4	4.1	7.7	3.0	3.8	3.3
Zambia						
PJ	150.8	62.8	20.4	11.2	31.3	87.9
%/Year	2.8	3.9	4.1	3.5	3.9	1.9
Zimbabwe						
PJ	244.1	117.2	24.9	65.8	26.4	126.9
%/Year	3.4	3.9	4.4	4.1	3.2	2.8
SADCC						
PJ	1456.3	305.9	57.3	93.3	155.2	1150.5
%/Year	3.0	4.0	4.7	4.0	3.7	2.6

[1] 1 PJ (peta-joule) = .034 million tonnes coal equivalent = .022
million tonnes oil equivalent.
[2]
    Final consumption only (e.g., coal figures do not include coal
    used for electricity generation).

 * Figures may not sum to totals due to rounding.

TABLE 5

SELECTED PER CAPITA ENERGY USE STATISTICS

	1980 Population (Million)	1980 GNP Per Capita (US $)	Annual Per Capita Energy Consumption						
try			Total (GJ)[1]	Commercial Fuels (%)	Tradi- tional Fuels (%)	Electri- city (KWH)	Coal (Tonnes)	Petro- leum (Tonnes)	Wood[2] (M^3)
la	7.08	440[3]	14.9	22.6	77.4	89	-	.07	.76
wana	0.81	910	27.3	43.9	56.1	577	.15	.12	.66
tho	1.34	420	18.0	21.4	78.6	69	.05	.05	.44
wi	6.16	230	26.8	5.7	94.3	59	.01	.02	1.16
mbique	10.47	250[3]	26.9	10.9	89.1	67	.02	.05	1.17
iland	0.56	680	42.8	40.0	60.0	815	.20	.18	.70
ania	17.93	280	24.5	8.5	91.5	36	-	.04	1.10
ia	5.77	560	26.1	41.7	58.3	988	.07	.12	1.10
abwe	7.40	630	33.0	48.0	52.0	943	.30	.08	.77
C	57.52	380	25.3	21.0	79.0	279	.06	.06	1.01

es: [1] 1 GJ (giga-joule) = 10^9 J = .034 tonnes coal equivalent = .022 tonnes oil equivalent.

[2] Total wood requirements (includes wood for charcoal production, construction, industrial purposes, and losses).

[3] 1979 Figure.

TABLE 6

1980 SECTORAL BREAKDOWN OF FINAL CONSUMPTION
(PJ and %)*

	Total	Urban HH's	Rural HH's	Agri- culture	Industry	Comm./ Inst.	Trans- portatio
Angola	105.5 PJ (100%)	6.5 (6)	52.3 (50)	1.8 (2)	28.7 (27)	9.3 (9)	7.0 (7)
Botswana	22.1 PJ (100%)	0.7 (3)	10.1 (46)	0.9 (4)	7.0 (32)	1.1 (5)	2.3 (10)
Lesotho	24.2 PJ (100%)	1.2 (5)	16.4 (68)	0.3 (1)	4.0 (17)	1.2 (5)	1.2 (5)
Malawi	165.2 PJ (100%)	4.1 (2)	63.7 (39)	55.7 (34)	37.3 (23)	0.7 -	3.7 (2)
Mozambique	281.7 PJ (100%)	8.9 (3)	206.2 (73)	3.7 (1)	46.8 (17)	3.9 (1)	12.2 (4)
Swaziland	23.9 PJ (100%)	0.7 (3)	4.5 (19)	0.7 (3)	14.1 (59)	.7 (3)	3.3 (14)
Tanzania	438.9 PJ (100%)	12.2 (3)	272.7 (62)	5.4 (1)	97.7 (22)	31.8 (7)	19.1 (4)
Zambia	150.8 PJ (100%)	15.4 (10)	58.0 (38)	1.2 (1)	54.3 (36)	5.5 (4)	16.3 (11)
Zimbabwe	244.1 PJ (100%)	10.0 (4)	102.3 (42)	17.5 (7)	77.9 (32)	10.3 (4)	26.0 (11)
SADCC	1456.3 PJ (100%)	59.7 (4)	786.2 (54)	87.7 (6)	367.8 (25)	64.5 (4)	91.1 (6)

*Figures may not sum to totals due to rounding.

The breakdown of total energy consumption into commercial and
traditional fuels is presented in Table 4 for each country, along
with the SADCC summation. Per capita energy statistics are
presented in Table 5, where we see that the average 1980
consumption per capita in the SADCC area was 279 KWH of
electricity, 60 kilograms of coal and petroleum, and 1 cubic
meter of wood.

While Tables 4 and 5 give the national and regional final energy
demand estimates broken down by type of fuel, Table 6 displays
the sectoral components of total requirements. There, it will be
seen that over one-half of SADCC energy consumption is in rural
households, primarily in the form of fuelwood. One quarter of
energy requirements service the industrial sector; here primarily
commercial fuels are consumed. The remaining requirements are
spread over the urban household (4 per cent), agriculture (6 per
cent), commercial/institutional (4 per cent), and transportation
(6 per cent) sectors.

The discussions above on SADCC-wide energy demands masks some
striking variations between the member countries. For example,
Table 5 displays the range in population (.56 million for
Swaziland to 17.93 million for Tanzania) and GNP per capita (US
$230 for Malawi to US $910 for Botswana). Total annual per capita
energy consumption is seen to vary substantially about the 25 GJ
SADCC average, with Angola and Lesotho at 14.9 and 18.0 GJ,
respectively, and Zimbabwe and Swaziland at 33.0 and 42.8 GJ,
respectively.

TABLE 7

1980 Per Capita Commercial Fuel Demand
(Kilogram Coal Equivalent)

Country	Per Capita Demand
Angola	114
Botswana	407
Lesotho	131
Malawi	51
Mozambique	100
Swaziland	581
Tanzania	71
Zambia	371
Zimbabwe	537
SADCC	180

The commercial fuel percentage of total consumption, which averages 21 per cent for SADCC, spans a range from around 6-10 per cent (Malawi, Tanzania and Mozambique) to over 40 per cent (Botswana, Swaziland, Zambia and Zimbabwe). Annual per capita electricity consumption varies by an order of magnitude with four countries in the 500 to 1000 KWH range (Botswana, Swaziland, Zambia and Zimbabwe) and the others all less than 100 KWH. Similarly, wide variation in the pattern of per capita coal and oil demand will be observed in Table 5. The per capita commercial fuel usage is shown in Table 7.

With respect to per capita wood consumption, Table 5 reveals a scatter around the SADCC average of 1 M^3 per capita. However, as stressed earlier, there is considerable uncertainty in these figures, and they are best considered indicative at the present time.

Turning from per capita comparative statistics to total national energy demands, we may derive from Table 4 the percentage breakdowns shown below in Table 8. These figures compound the variations in population with those in per capita consumption. The importance of Zimbabwe and Zambia in regional commercial fuel consumption is due to their relatively high per capita levels, while Botswana and Swaziland, despite their high per capita levels, contribute only 3 per cent each due to their relatively low populations.

Referring to Table 6, it will be observed that the sectoral decompositon of total national demand also exhibits variation across countries. For instance, the rural household demand, which accounts for 54 per cent of the SADCC total, ranges from 19 per cent in Swaziland to 73 per cent in Mozambique. This spread is partially explained by both the degree of urbanization (see Table 9 below) and the relative contribution of other sectors in each country's economic structure. Other factors influencing the sectoral contribution to demand are the intensity of usage at the end-use (e.g., inefficient wood stoves require four to five times more fuel than kerosene stoves), industrial process mix, transportation fleet characteristics, degree of electrification, and appliance saturation in buildings.

The energy demand situation across the SADCC countries shows certain common patterns along with considerable country-specific diversity. In considering options for mutual cooperation, these special characteristics will need to be addressed in the context of each country's development trajectory as well as regional self-sufficiency objectives. The discussion of energy demand has

TABLE 8

Country Demands As Percent Of SADCC Total

Country	Commercial Total	Traditional Fuels	Fuels
Angola	7.2%	7.8%	7.1%
Botswana	1.5	3.2	1.1
Lesotho	1.7	1.7	1.7
Malawi	11.3	3.1	13.5
Mozambique	19.3	10.0	21.8
Swaziland	1.6	3.1	1.2
Tanzania	30.1	12.3	34.9
Zambia	10.4	20.5	7.6
Zimbabwe	16.8	38.3	11.0
SADCC	100.0%	100.0%	100.0%

TABLE 9

Urban Population As A Percentage Of Total Population

Country	Urban Percentage
Angola	21.1
Botswana	13.4
Lesotho	9.4
Malawi	7.3
Mozambique	7.8
Swaziland	14.7
Tanzania	7.3
Zambia	42.0
Zimbabwe	22.7
SADCC	14.7

been static to this point. The discussion of opportunities for SADCC energy initiatives is best put in the dynamic perspective of long-range energy requirements, a subject to which we now turn.

2.C Long-Range Projections

Projections of energy demands for each of the demand categories have been developed for each member country. Again we restrict the discussion here to a summary of the results, while referring the interested reader to the annex for the details.

The key demographic assumptions employed in developing the long-range projections are presented in Table 10. The SADCC-wide average annual growth rate of population is taken at 3.2 per cent/year, with the country-specific growth rates ranging from 2.6 to 3.5 per cent/year. The rate of growth projected for urban population in the SADCC region (5.6 per cent/year) is about twice that projected for rural population (2.6 per cent/year). The ratio of urban to rural growth rates is higher still in Angola (3.1), Swaziland (2.5), and Zambia (3.8).

These demographic trends have implications for the future mix of energy requirements. The urbanization phenomena suggest that growth in commercial fuel requirements is likely to exceed growth in traditional fuel requirements. However, in those countries where charcoal is used, there is a compensating factor with

TABLE 10

DEMOGRAPHIC/ECONOMIC ASSUMPTIONS
(Populations and Households in Millions)

	1980	1990	2000	Average Annual Growth Rate (%/Year)
Angola				
Total Population	7.08	9.28	12.38	2.8
Urban Population	1.49	2.62	4.37	5.5
Rural Population	5.59	6.66	8.01	1.8
Urban Households	0.25	0.44	0.73	5.5
Rural Households	0.70	0.83	1.00	1.8
GDP Index	1.0	1.34	1.81	3.0
Botswana				
Total Population	0.81	1.12	1.60	3.5
Urban Population	0.11	0.19	0.34	5.8
Rural Population	0.70	0.93	1.26	3.0
Urban Households	0.024	0.042	0.076	5.8
Rural Households	0.12	0.15	0.21	3.0
GDP Index	1.0	1.41	1.99	3.5
Lesotho				
Total Population	1.34	1.73	2.22	2.6
Urban Population	0.126	0.19	0.33	4.9
Rural Population	1.22	1.54	1.89	2.2
Urban Households	0.030	0.045	0.078	4.9
Rural Households	0.24	0.30	0.37	2.2
GDP Index	1.0	1.29	1.67	2.6
Malawi				
Total Population	6.16	8.63	12.01	3.4
Urban Population	0.45	0.84	1.45	6.1
Rural Population	5.71	7.79	10.55	3.1
Urban Households	0.10	0.20	0.34	6.1
Rural Households	0.95	1.30	1.76	3.1
GDP Index	1.0	1.34	1.81	3.0
Mozambique				
Total Population	10.47	13.89	18.70	2.9
Urban Population	0.81	1.46	2.48	5.8
Rural Population	9.66	12.43	16.22	2.6
Urban Households	0.18	0.33	0.56	5.8
Rural Households	2.26	2.91	3.80	2.6
GDP Index	1.0	1.34	1.81	3.0

	1980	1990	2000	Average Annual Growth Rate %/Year
Swaziland				
Total Population	0.557	0.754	1.020	3.1
Urban Population	0.082	0.169	0.262	5.9
Rural Population	0.475	0.585	0.758	2.4
Urban Households	0.018	0.0375	0.0582	5.9
Rural Households	0.054	0.066	0.086	2.4
GDP Index	1.0	1.34	1.81	3.0
Tanzania				
Total Population	17.93	24.77	34.03	3.3
Urban Population	1.31	2.50	4.26	6.1
Rural Population	16.62	22.27	29.77	3.0
Urban Households	0.29	0.56	0.95	6.1
Rural Households	2.77	3.71	4.96	3.0
GDP Index	1.0	1.34	1.81	3.0
Zambia				
Total Population	5.77	8.08	11.28	3.4
Urban Population	2.42	4.14	6.82	5.3
Rural Population	3.35	3.94	4.46	1.4
Urban Households	0.30	0.51	0.77	5.3
Rural Households	0.58	0.68	0.77	1.4
GDP Index	1.00	1.41	1.99	3.5
Zimbabwe				
Total Population	7.40	10.49	14.73	3.5
Urban Population	1.68	2.94	4.92	5.5
Rural Population	5.72	7.55	9.81	2.7
Urban Households	0.26	0.46	0.77	5.5
Rural Households	0.84	1.12	1.45	2.7
GDP Index	1.0	1.42	2.03	3.6

Notes:

Populations from United Nations Medium Variant Projections of Population Growth. Field team estimate of urban/rural split for Swaziland and Lesotho.

Household size from field reports were available (Zambia, Botswana, Zimbabwe, Angola, Mozambique) or generic persons per household (4.3 and 6 for urban and rural, respectively).

respect to total wood requirements, (see Table 11 below) since, on a volume basis, there is something like an 8 to 1 conversion ratio of wood to charcoal. Charcoal is used primarily in urban households and, it appears, north of the Zambeze River, although there are exceptions, such as southern Mozambique. Thus, Angola and Zambia, with relatively large urban populations (see Table 9), are seen in Table 11 to have the largest percentage of charcoal usage. This has significant implications for the pattern of pressure put on wood resources, a subject to which we shall return below.

Another significant parameter affecting long-range patterns is the assumed growth in economic output. The Gross Domestic Product (GDP) growth rates utilized in the projections are shown in Table 10. The assumptions are guided by population growth rates and project team judgments; as such they should be considered scenarios rather than predictions.

The projected average annual growth rates of final fuel demand for the period 1980-2000 were presented below the absolute 1980 consumption estimates in Table 4. The SADCC-wide growth rate for total demand, commercial fuel demand, and traditional demand are seen to be 3 per cent/year, 4 per cent/year, and 2.6 per cent/year, respectively, reflecting the underlying assumptions on economic and population growth, urbanization, and modernization. The play of these factors in the individual country setting, along with the variations in the current sectoral and fuel mix structure of demand, lead to the growth rates for the nine member countries shown in Table 4.

Within the commercial fuel category, electricity grows the fastest at 4.7 per cent/year due in part to modest increases in assumed electrification levels (increases in household hook-ups by 5 to 10 per cent above 1980 levels by the year 2000). Coal usage increases more rapidly than petroleum (4 per cent/year versus 3.7 per cent/year) due to projected coal switching in boilers in coal-rich countries.

Figure 2 shows graphically the projected 20-year growth in fuel requirements within SADCC as a whole and for each member country.

The long-range forecast of national consumption is reported in Output Table 5 in the Annex. The detailed components of demand growth by sector, subsector, and fuel will be found for each country in Output Table 6 in the Annex. The consumption for 1990 across all categories is in Output Table 4.

TABLE 11

CHARCOAL AS PERCENTAGE OF TRADITIONAL FUEL CONSUMPTION

Country	Charcoal Percentage
Angola	16%
Botswana	-
Lesotho	-
Malawi	1%
Mozambique	5%
Swaziland	-
Tanzania	4%
Zambia	21%
Zimbabwe	-

Figure 2

SADCC GROWTH IN FINAL ENERGY CONSUMPTION

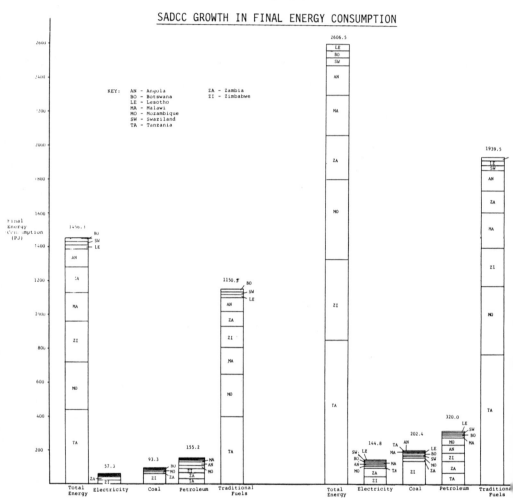

3. ENERGY SUPPLY

In the previous discussion, the current pattern of end-use energy consumption was summarized for each SADCC country, and a scenario for the long-range evolution of final fuel demand developed. This section reviews the complementary issues of the sources of energy supply, the physical resource base, and the prospects for balancing regional fuel demand against regional resources.

The material is organized by resource type rather than by country, since the main thrust of the exercise in this section is to explore the physical basis for regional self-sufficiency (institutional and economic preconditions are discussed in subsequent sections). We first treat the availability of commercial fuel resources (oil, coal, and electricity), and go on to note that currently planned energy resource development alone is likely to be more than sufficient for the region if coordinated interchange between supply and demand centres proves feasible.

The SADCC region is fortunate in having an abundant quantity and diversity of exploitable resources. If spatial, financial, and institutional hurdles can be overcome, it appears that the physical resource base is adequate to support a development and modernization pace beyond that assumed in our demand forecast scenarios.

In fact, the SADCC region is already engaged in a number of exchanges of energy commodities, both within its boundaries and beyond. Figure 3 illustrates the current international energy links in which SADCC countries are involved. The map illustrates the current minimal pattern of internal energy trade links within the region. As oil flows out from the west coast and in from the east and south, electricity imports (except for power sharing arrangements between Zambia and Zimbabwe at the Kariba complex on their common border) are only through South Africa, and coal trade is currently dominated by exports outside the region. On the other hand, the current infrastructure of refineries, pipelines, railways, port facilities, and electric grids are the embryonic building blocks for stronger energy linkages in the region.

With respect to the non-commercial resources (primarily woody biomass), we shall note that serious local resource shortages have already appeared. These are likely to deepen in the absence of fuelwood programmes to increase the supply of sustainable biomass yields, to improve the conversion efficiency of end-use devices, and to accelerate switching to other fuels. Much work needs to be done to identify the detailed character of the

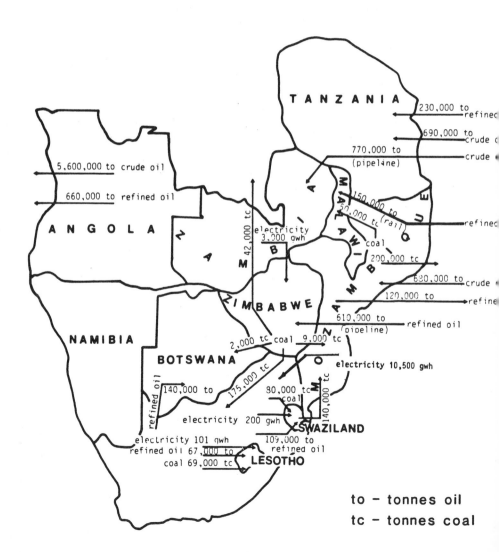

- 28 -

Figure 3

CURRENT INTERNATIONAL ENERGY LINKS

to – tonnes oil
tc – tonnes coal

problem for each country and to devise effective and ongoing
initiatives for addressing this growing problem which threatens
rural economic stability and development. As we shall discuss,
there is an important regional role here as well, in the possible
provision of alternative fuels, and in mounting joint efforts in
aspects of fuelwood programme development from which efficiencies
and economies could be derived.

By devoting less attention to other renewable resources options -
e.g., wind power, solar applications, biogas, biomass-derived
alcohols, and small hydro - we do not intend to deny the important
role that certain subsets of these can play in each country.
Indeed, there appears to be an important SADCC coordinative role
in centralizing research, development, training, and
demonstration efforts, and optimizing the dissemination of
findings, technologies, and programme opportunities, to avoid an
unnecessary duplication of efforts. We shall return to this theme
later, but we will now focus on those energy forms that are
likely to remain predominant up to the end of this century.

3.A Petroleum and Natural Gas

We begin by summarizing the current situation with respect to the
uses and sources of oil. The petroleum balance for 1980 is shown
in Table 12 for each country and is summed to yield SADCC totals.
The table lists separately the requirements for crude (as an
input to refineries) and the requirements for refined petroleum
products (final demands plus refinery and distribution losses).

Along with the national requirements, estimates of production,
imports, and exports are given. These satisfy the identity:

Requirements = Production + Imports - Exports. The petroleum
flows are shown schematically in Figure 4.
Angola is the only member country which currently produces crude.
While there are preliminary indications of possible oil deposits
in other SADCC countries, it would be prudent for planning
purposes at this time, to assume that the output will come
entirely from Angola. As Table 12 indicates, Angolan crude oil
production (6.8 million tonnes/year) was three times the crude
imports in the rest of the SADCC region (2.19 million
tonnes/year). After subtracting its own requirements, available
crude from Angola was still 2.5 times these imports. In 1980, the
foreign exchange cost to the importing SADCC countries was almost
US $500 million for crude alone.

With regard to refined oil, the situation in 1980 was as follows.
The region's refinery output (3.26 million tonnes/year) was 86
per cent of requirements (3.78 million tonnes/year). However,
one-third of this output was exported to the rest-of-the-world,
implying that 42 per cent of refined product requirements had to
be imported with additional foreign exchange burdens.

TABLE 12

PETROLEUM RESOURCE SUMMARY
(Million Tonnes/Year)

Country	1980				1990			
	Produc-tion	Imports	Exports	Require-ments	Produc-tion	Imports	Exports	Require-ments
Angola								
Crude*	6.80	–	5.57	1.23	10.10	–	7.31	2.79
Refined	1.16	–	.66	.50	2.63	–	1.88	.75
Botswana								
Crude	–	–	–	–	–	–	–	–
Refined	–	.14	–	.14	–	.15	–	.15
Lesotho								
Crude	–	–	–	–	–	–	–	–
Refined	–	.07	–	.07	–	.09	–	.09
Malawi								
Crude	–	–	–	–	–	–	–	–
Refined	–	.16	–	.16	–	.22	–	.22
Mozambique								
Crude	–	.68	–	.68	–	.79	–	.79
Refined	.66	.14	.26	.54	.77	.21	.26	.72
Swaziland								
Crude	–	–	–	–	–	–	–	–
Refined	–	.11	–	.11	–	.15	–	.15
Tanzania								
Crude	–	.69	–	.69	–	.73	–	.73
Refined	.66	.37	.13	.90	.70	.67	.13	1.24
Zambia								
Crude	–	.82	–	.82	–	1.09	–	1.09
Refined	.78	–	.03	.75	1.04	–	.08	.96
Zimbabwe								
Crude	–	–	–	–	–	–	–	–
Refined	–	.61	–	.61	–	.84	–	.84
SADCC								
Crude	6.80	2.19	5.57	3.42	10.10	2.61	7.31	5.40
Refined	3.26	1.60	1.08	3.78	5.14	2.33	2.35	5.12

*
Angola's resource base and near term production potential for crude oil has been estimated
to be 400 million tonnes total recoverable (technologically exploitable) resources and
2500 million tonnes overall potential (theoretically feasible).

Figure 4

PETROLEUM BALANCES

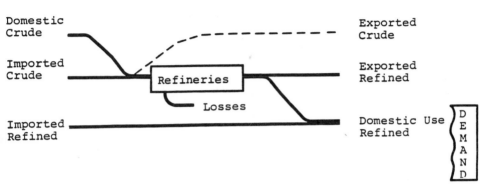

The effect is skewed across member countries. Certain of these countries (Botswana, Lesotho, Swaziland, Malawi, and Zimbabwe) which have no operating refineries are completely dependent on imports, the first three from South Africa and the last two from beyond the continent. Mozambique, Zambia and Tanzania have refinery capacity, but must import all their crude inputs. Additionally, in the case of Mozambique and Tanzania, substantial refined exports occur (primarily fuel oil), due to the mismatch between refinery output mix and national end-use demand mix. Thus, these exports are complemented by the importation of lighter petroleum products. Finally, of course, Angola is a large exporter of both crude and refined oil products.

The refineries in Mozambique, Tanzania, Zambia, and Angola were operating at 86, 95, 75 and 83 per cent of their respective capacities in 1980. Zambia's refinery, supplied with crude through the TAZAMA pipeline from Dar es Salaam, was utilized almost exclusively for local demand and met the country's entire needs for refined products. Angola also satisfied its national demand from its own refinery but exported 660 thousand tonnes of refined products in 1980; and still it had excess capacity. Tanzania was the largest importer of refined products in the region in 1980, despite using nearly all of its refinery capacity. Mozambique had to import over 25 per cent of its refined product needs in 1980, while running its refinery with 14 per cent unutilized capacity.

By 1990 the relative positions within the region are expected to remain as they are now (see Table 12): Angola as the only producer, with output roughly twice the requirements of the nine SADCC member nations.* Mozambique, Tanzania and Zambia are expected to maintain their present refinery capacity and, with the exception of a small export increase for Zambia, all three are expected to supply their domestic markets using 100 per cent capacity refinery throughput, with Mozambique and Tanzania requiring supplementary imports. No refinery capacity installations are anticipated for the five countries which currently have none. Angola is projected to expand its refinery capacity by 166 per cent, from 1.5 to 4.0 million tonnes per year by 1990, with exports of refined products increasing threefold over 1980 levels.

---

* The 1990 crude oil production projections for Angola may prove to be far too low. Indeed, there is a possibility that 10.5 million tonnes of output will be reached in 1982 (Economist Intelligence Unit, Quarterly Energy Review, Third Quarter, 1982). Increased output estimates would imply greater Angolan exports to the rest-of-the-world but alter none of the basic findings and recommendations on regional energy issues.

Import of crude as a percentage of crude requirements in SADCC is projected to decrease from 64 per cent to 48 per cent, over the 1980 to 1990 period. However, outside of Angola, crude imports will increase by about 20 per cent if no additional oil fields are developed. Refined imports will increase regionally by nearly 50 per cent according to Table 12.

Although successful exploitation of oil resources outside Angola would require an adjustment to these figures, the overall supply/demand picture in SADCC is unlikely to change dramatically over the next ten years. It is worth noting, however, that exploratory drilling in both onshore and offshore blocks is expected soon in Mozambique. The geology of the onshore Rovuma basin is considered promising by experts. Three onshore and one offshore exploration programmes are expected to be launched soon in Tanzania.
While these activities cannot be taken to mean that oil will either be found or that wells will be producing by 1990, it is important to stress that the geological work done to date justifies these exploration programmes.

There is also potential for utilizing previously unexploited natural gas deposits. The prognosis for natural gas consumption as a substitute for other fuels was considered too uncertain at this time for inclusion in the projection scenarios. However, several interesting prospects are notable.

In Angola, substantial recoverable natural gas resources (about 1500 billion cubic meters) are available. The amount of natural gas escaping from the oil fields during crude oil extraction has been at the rate of about 1 billion cubic meters per year (on an energy content basis this is over 10 per cent of the region's total commercial fuel requirement). In the past almost all of this was wasted ("flared"), with a small amount pumped back into the wells to help "lift" more oil. There are currently plans to increase the amount of the natural gas used for pumping, and to use some of it to produce LPG for household consumption.

Tanzania is currently developing its natural gas fields at Songo Songo, and plans to build a fertilizer plant using natural gas as a feedstock. Production is estimated to reach one million cubic meters per day (14 PJ/year). Mozambique has natural gas deposits in the Pande area of up to about 100 billion cubic meters and some gas fields elsewhere. Appraisal of commercial utilization feasibility is continuing.

3.B Coal

The coal resource endowment in the SADCC region is substantial, albeit unevenly distributed and exploited. Currently proven reserves (those considered technically and economically recoverable) are estimated at over 11 billion tonnes, as compared to a 1980 SADCC-wide consumption of 4.32 million tonnes. The area is already a net exporter of coal, and the prospects are for coal to be an increasingly important source of foreign exchange.

The coal situation is summarised in Table 13. Resource estimates are given for each country, along with energy balances for our base year (1980) and a selected future year (1990). These are summed to SADCC regional totals at the bottom of the table.
Coal deposits have been identified in seven of the nine member countries. Coal is currently being mined in six of the countries, with an estimated total production in 1980 of 4.58 million tonnes. Coal has not been found to date in Angola and Lesotho and has not yet been exploited in Malawi.* World geological resources are dominated by three countries (the U.S., the U.S.S.R., and China) which together possess nearly 90 per cent of all resources and 60 per cent of recoverable reserves. Nevertheless, the world average per capita coal reserves (130 tce) is less than the SADCC per capita figure (200 tce).

The region's physical resource base is sufficient to meet vastly greater coal consumption and production levels. But the contrast between the world average per capita coal production (about 600 kgCe) and the SADCC average per capita coal production (80 kgCE), reflects the early stage of coal resource development in the region. Indeed, coal output is projected to increase by a factor of 3.5 over the 1980-1990 period, equivalent to an average growth rate of 13 per cent/year.

The projected coal balances for 1990 are presented in Table 13. Major increases in output are shown for the six current producing countries, with the increase in Botswana production accounting for half of the SADCC-wide increase. At the same time, the requirements for coal within the region are anticipated to increase at 5.1 per cent/year to a 1990 figure of 6.4 million tonnes. This growth rate is nearly two percentage points higher than total energy demand growth rates, and one percentage point higher than total commercial energy growth rates. This reflects a trend toward greater usage of coal (as opposed to liquid fuels) as a source of thermal energy for industrial processes, space and water heating, and electricity generation.

---

*   In Malawi, due to the low quality sub-bituminous coal found and long transportation distances from the most promising deposit at Ngana, the cost of delivered coal may not be competitive with continued imports. The likelihood of near-term coal development must be considered small therefore.

- 35 -

TABLE 13

COAL RESOURCE SUMMARY
(Million Tonnes)

Country	Resource Base* Total	Resource Base* Proven Reserves	1980 Pro-duction	1980 Imports	1980 Exports	1980 Require-ments	1990 Pro-duction	1990 Imports	1990 Exports	1990 Require-ments
Angola	0	0	0	0	0	0	0	0	0	0
Botswana	160,000	7,000	.37	.02	0	.39	6.0	0	5.45	.55
Lesotho	0	0	0	.07	0	.07	0	.11	0	.11
Malawi	?	12	0	.05	0	.05	0	.07	0	.07
Mozambique	395	240	.36	.14	.25	.25	2.0	0	1.73	.27
Swaziland	5,020	2,020	.18	.08	.14	.12	1.5	0	1.31	.19
Tanzania	360	35	.01	-	0	.01	.34	0	0	.34
Zambia	130	32	.40	0	0	.40	1.9	0	1.34	.56
Zimbabwe	29,200	2,200	3.26	0	.23	3.03	4.6	0	.29	4.31
SADCC	195,105+	11,509	4.58	.36	.62	4.32	16.34	.18	10.12	6.40

*Sources: Field Reports, UN 1979 Yearbook of World Energy Statistics, 1981, and World Bank "Coal Development Potential and Prospects in the Developing Countries," 1979.

Despite the rapid increase in regional coal consumption, the 1990
coal balance shows net exports to the rest of the world rising
from 0.3 million tce in 1980 to about 10.0 million tce in 1990.
Coal could, in this scenario, be an important source of foreign
exchange, paying for all (Botswana, Swaziland) or a sizeable
fraction (Mozambique, Zambia) of future oil import bills.
Achievement of these production targets, of course, is predicated
on the continued strength of the world coal market, and the
assurance of an adequate transportation network in the region, in
particular, with the rehabilitation and upgrading of the
railways. We shall return to a discussion of issues in regional
coal development in later sections.

3.C Electricity

In section 2, the current and projected demands for electricity
within the SADCC region as a whole and for each member country
were discussed. Electricity demands have been expressed in terms
of national total and national per capita consumption in Tables 4
and 5 respectively. A wide variation in both of these amongst
member countries was noted. Total consumption in 1980 (including
transmission and distribution losses) is seen to range from about
101 GWH (101 million KWH) to 7288 GWH in Table 14 and per capita
final consumption in 1980 from 36 KWH to 988 KWH in Table 5. In
this section we shall describe the electricity generation systems
within SADCC, both current and planned, and examine the potential
for additional supplies of electricity from hydro development.

Table 14 summarizes the electricity supply/demand configuration
within the SADCC area for 1980 and 1990, and the potential for
additional hydro power.* The first seven columns of numbers
summarize the 1980 experience. There it can be seen that a grand
total of 28,644 GWH was generated as compared with 17,130 GWH of
consumption (final demand plus transmission/distribution losses).
Total generation was about 94 per cent hydro and 6 per cent from
other sources (mostly coal), while total capacity was 81 per cent
hydro and 19 per cent from other sources (primarily coal- and
oil-fired, and some residue-fired). The detailed breakdowns for
each country will be found in Output Table 7 in the Annex.

A number of striking features emerge from these aggregates.
First, SADCC as a whole already generates much more electricity
than it consumes, by about 67 per cent (or 11,514 GWH), and its

_____

* The 1980 figures in Table 14 and the Annex Output Table reflect
a discrepancy in the electrical energy imports of Zimbabwe from
Zambia, with Zimbabwe reporting a figure of 1756 GWH and Zambia
reporting 3136 GWH.

TABLE 14

ELECTRICITY SUPPLY AND DEMAND SUMMARY

| | 1980 | | | | | | | 1990 | | | | | | | | | |
| | Generation (GWH) | | | Consumption* (GWH) | Capacity (MW) | | | Generation (GWH) | | | Consumption (GWH) | Capacity (MW) | | | Generation at full Output (GWH) + | Additional Hydro Potential | |
	Hydro	Other	Total		Hydro	Other	Total	Hydro	Other	Total		Hydro	Other	Total		Capacity (MW)	Generation (GWH)
Angola	675	15	690	690	287	185	472	1297	0	1297	1297	1287	185	1472	5812	14458	73458
Botswana	0	510	510	510	0	108	108	0	767	767	767	0	219	219	981	3000	15768
Lesotho	0	0	0	101	0	0	0	0	0	0	187	0	0	0	0	0	0
Malawi	383	6	389	389	125	23	148	712	3	715	715	164	23	187	1009	336	2060
Mozambique	11010	243	11253	751	2151	158	2309	12244	96	12340	1540	3381	158	3539	17340	8756	44487
Swaziland	122	171	293	500	21	45	66	256	341	597	802	43	63	106	597	0	0
Tanzania	486	268	754	754	150	102	252	858	855	1713	1713	280	396	676	1713	2100	6438
Zambia	9202	81	9283	6147	1669	90	1759	9158	12	9170	9170	2419	90	2509	15057	0	0
Zimbabwe	5000	472	5472	7288	666	485	1151	9538	1641	11179	11179	1266	1765	3031	17269	1489	11217
SADCC	26878	1766	28644	17130	5069	1196	6265	34063	3715	37778	27370	8840	2899	11739	59778	30139	153428

* Consumption includes transmission/distribution losses.

+ With maximum output from hydro and coal facilities.

total capacity of 6265 MW is more than 100 per cent greater than the sum of the member country peak demand requirements. Second, hydropower dominates both generation and installed capacity, with the hydro capacity having a much greater average utilization than other forms (average capacity factor* was 61 per cent for hydro, 17 per cent for other), because of low hydro production costs.

While the SADCC-wide electricity supply aggregates illuminate the regional resource picture and indicate regional self-sufficiency, there is a wide variation among the countries. The average of 81 per cent regional hydro capacity embodies a range from 0 per cent in Botswana (which has 64 per cent coal capacity) to about 95 per cent in Zambia and Mozambique, with Swaziland at 32 per cent, Zimbabwe at 58 per cent, Angola and Tanzania at 60 per cent and Malawi at 84 per cent. Almost 90 per cent of all existing hydro capacity in SADCC is located in three adjacent countries, Zimbabwe, Mozambique, and Zambia, primarily in the Kariba and Cabora Bassa facilities. The major coal-fired generation is found in Botswana (380 GWH or 75 per cent of its total) and Zimbabwe where 532 GWH contributes only 7.5 per cent of total national generation. Oil-fired generation is greatest in Botswana (130 GWH or 25 per cent of its total) and in Tanzania (268 GWH or 36 per cent of its total).

Despite the overall surplus power within SADCC, some of the member countries engage in imports and exports of electricity both amongst themselves and outside SADCC (the links were displayed in Figure 3). Lesotho and Swaziland are at present heavily dependent upon the Republic of South Africa for electricity. Lesotho, with no installed capacity within its national boundaries, imports all of its electricity, 101 GWH, from South Africa, while Swaziland meets about 40 per cent of its requirements (or about 200 GWH) from South Africa. Both Zimbabwe and Mozambique, which have sufficient internal capacity, also import electricity. Zimbabwe imports about 24 per cent of its requirements from Zambia, consequently using its existing coal capacity at a low capacity factor (about 12 per cent), while Mozambique imports only about 3 per cent of its requirements.

The bulk of the electrical energy generated in excess of requirements in 1980, fully 10,800 GWH, is sent outside the SADCC region, in particular as Mozambican exports to the Republic of South Africa. While this has been the experience in the past, this generation is in principle a SADCC resource, potentially available for use within Mozambique and neighbouring SADCC countries Such potential, however, can only be realized if

---

* Actual annual generation divided by full-output generation (rated capacity times 8760 hours/year).

transmission links between some of the SADCC countries are established. In Section 4.D, issues concerning the development of stronger SADCC electrical interconnections are raised.

The existing capacity expansion plans within SADCC must be considered in relation to the projected growth in demand. Looking again at Table 14, we find that by 1990 demand is projected to grow by about 60 per cent to 27,370 GWH, while generation is anticipated to grow by 32 per cent to 37,778 GWH. It is worth re-emphasizing that there are great uncertainties in long-range forecasts of both demand and planned construction. Assuming that all of this generation is available within SADCC, regional self-sufficiency can be maintained. Similarly, by 1990 installed capacity is expected to be 11,739 MW, an increase of about 87 per cent, whereas the sum of peak demands will be 4929 MW, an increase of about 60 per cent. Based on these figures, overall capacity would increase more than demand. Thus, implicit in these numbers is a potential underutilization of planned capacity.

Planned new hydro capacity in Angola includes an additonal 260 MW at Cambambe Dam on the Cuanza River, 150 MW at Lomgum Dam on the Catumbela River, and 160 MW on the Calonga River. In Zimbabwe an additional 600 MW hydro capacity is planned in the Kariba North extension, and an additional 1280 MW of coal-fired capacity is planned (at Wankie). In Zambia 750 MW of new hydro capacity is planned. An additional 1230 MW hydro capacity is planned in Mozambique in Cabora Bassa 11. Planned hydro capacity within SADCC will be rather underutilized by 1990, given the demand projections. In Angola, for example, if only 1000 MW of about 6000 MW contemplated is built by 1990 (as is assumed here) hydro capacity will operate at an estimated 12 per cent capacity factor. In the other countries with planned hydro capacity the utilization would be about or below 50 per cent, except for Zimbabwe at 86 per cent and Swaziland at 68 per cent. However, the former would have underutilized coal facilities and the latter would remain dependent on imports.

All SADCC countries with the exception of Swaziland and Lesotho are anticipated to generate enough electricity to meet national requirements. Lesotho will need to import all of its 187 GWH and Swaziland will need to import 205 GWH, about one-quarter of its requirements. If part of the surplus generation available within SADCC, particularly from Mozambique, could be made available, imports from South Africa would be unnecessary. (The 1980 imports by South Africa from Cabora Bassa in Mozambique, were very much larger than the export of electricity from South Africa to Lesotho, Swaziland and Botswana). Moreover, the planned capacity in some countries will be underutilized even without intra-SADCC exchanges. For example, in Zimbabwe the low utilization of 485 MW of coal-fired capacity in 1980 was related to taking imports from

Zambia. However, by 1990, 600 MW of new hyro capacity and 1280 MW of new coal-fired capacity will be installed according to current plans.

Total capacity would be 3031 MW as compared with 1657 MW peak demand. As a consequence, even without imports, the utilization or capacity factor of its coal plants will average only about 11 per cent. Thus, on the basis of its own needs alone, Zimbabwe appears to be overbuilding generating capacity. On the other hand, Tanzania will still be utilizing oil to generate about 184 GWH (11 per cent of its needs) and will build coal-fired generation which will supply 671 GWH (39 per cent of its needs). Botswana will expand its coal capacity from 69 to 180 MW, thus reducing its need to use oil-fired generation by 1990. The potential exists for reducing both coal and oil use by importing surplus hydro-electricity from other countries. Moreover, it is possible that some planned generation capacity could be deferred, if existing and planned surplus capacity can be made available across national boundaries.

Examining Table 14 again, it can be seen that if planned hydro and coal-fired capacity generated at full output (maximum feasible capacity factor) in 1990, total SADCC generation would be roughly 60,000 GWH as compared with 27,370 GWH demand. Substantial surpluses would arise in Angola (4515 GWH), Mozambique (15,800 GWH), Zambia (5887 GWH), and Zimbabwe (6090 GWH). If electricity demands in these countries were to grow much faster than is currently projected, e.g. with greater urban and industrial development or rural and periurban electrification, there is an enormous potential available to meet these needs if the necessary grid extensions can be made. On the other hand, looking again at the situation on a SADCC-wide basis, such planned surpluses could in principle be utilized cooperatively if economies can be achieved and institutional conditions permit. An important beginning is being made with the proposed linkage between Mutare in Zimbabwe and the surplus capacity available near Chimoio, in Mozambique.

The full resource potential within the SADCC region is far more vast than current planned expansion. A total additional hydro capacity of about 30,000 MW, and generation of 153,000 GWH could be realized ultimately if economic conditions are favourable. Some of this potential is under investigation at this time. For example, sixty possible hydropower sites have been identified in Mozambique and some are being considered for implementation. Similarly, in Angola more than 5000 MW of the full additional hydro resource potential of 14,458 MW have been identified, primarily on the Cuanza River. In Tanzania 2100 MW potential at Stieglers Gorge has been identified, and studies, tender documents, and access roads have been completed. In Zimbabwe

several thousand MW of new hydro are under investigation.
Finally, the potential for geothermal energy in Tanzania and
Mozambique along the East African rift system could be further
explored.

3.D Regional Sufficiency of Commercial Fuels

Ignoring, for a moment, spatial, financial, and institutional
impediments to meeting the evolving regional fuel demands with
anticipated regional supplies, a striking conclusion is reached.
On a physical basis, the energy foundation of the region is
robust. The long-term availability of large surpluses of modern
fuel forms in the SADCC area as a whole suggests that, in
principle, with adequate regional cooperation, the energy sector
could well be an engine for economic development rather than the
brake it is in many less well endowed countries. Even the
aforementioned potentially formidable impediments can be
overcome. One possibility, concerning foreign exchange
bottlenecks, may be to link partial trade agreements with cross
border energy supplies. Barter exchange can also be used to
facilitate regional linkages.

The surplus of commercial fuels on an aggregate energy basis is
presented for 1990 in Table 15. The regional requirements and
production capability are drawn from the previous discussion. The
surpluses of electricity, coal, and crude oil are massive: 118
per cent of requirements for electricity, 155 per cent of
requirements for coal, and 87 per cent of requirements for crude
oil. Taking these three resources together, the region will
produce over twice the quantity needed to meet projected internal
requirements. Additionally, the gross output of refinery capacity
is seen to be adequate to meet regional demands.

It is worth remembering that these impressive surpluses are based
on projected energy production capability not potential
economically exploitable resources. For each fuel type there is
an abundance of additional promising potential in the region for
hydro, coal, oil and natural gas development beyond the projected
figures for 1990.

At the level of the physical availability of commercial fuels in
the region, then, there is ample opportunity for regional
self-sufficiency.
However, this physical supply/demand match in the aggregate masks
a number of country-specific and subregional problems. Among
these are fuel supplies within countries and subregions of the
area, the technical and economic feasibility of developing and
upgrading transportation and distribution networks to better link
source centres with use centres, and the need to create
institutional arrangements which would be effective in ensuring
mutual benefits to all countries.

TABLE 15

1990 SADCC-WIDE ENERGY SURPLUSES

(PJ/Year)

	Requirements	Production	Surplus
Electricity	98.5	215.2*	116.7
Coal	187.6	478.9	291.3
Refined Oil	232.3	233.2	0.9
Crude Oil	245.0	458.2	213.2

*Maximum output of all hydro and coal facilities

1 PJ = (10^{15} joules) = .022 million toe = .034 million tce = 277.7 GWH

On the other hand, the existence of energy surpluses in the
region does put such issues as energy programme coordination
squarely on the agenda. The first criterion for cooperative
long-range energy development is satisfied: the region will have
sufficient economically-viable commercial resources to satisfy
its projected needs or, for that matter, to sustain large scale
programmes that accelerate the energy intensiveness of regional
development.

3.E Biomass

The prognosis just discussed for regional surpluses in commercial
fuels contrasts sharply with the outlook for traditional fuel.
Many people in the region are already experiencing difficulties
in obtaining sufficient and readily available supplies of wood.
Although commercial fuel prospects are rightfully considered to
be of special interest given their role in meeting development
and modernization goals, the importance of traditional fuels in
the rural sector cannot be overlooked. We have already seen that
traditional fuels (wood, agricultural residue, dung) currently
supply fully 79 per cent of fuel demand for energy within SADCC.
Although the expected growth rate in the use of traditional fuels
is somewhat less than that for total energy requirements (Table
4), because of urbanization and modern sector development,
nevertheless, the projections reported in the Annex indicate that
its proportion of final demand will still be above 70 per cent in
the year 2000.

Wood and other biomass fuels comprise 50-95 per cent of total
annual energy consumption in the SADCC countries. Wood, charcoal,
crop-wastes and dung are used domestically for cooking,
space-heating and other household tasks, even for lighting. The
average consumption per person is 0.5-1.5 M^3 of wood per year.
There is a limit to how far from home it is possible to gather
wood (about 10 km) without it becoming extremely burdensome and
time consuming to the family; nevertheless many people in the
region are obliged to travel very long distances in their search
for fuel. Similarly, pack-animal or truck transport of wood or
charcoal becomes totally uneconomic beyond certain distances.
This means that under steady harvesting, wood can become in short
supply or entirely absent around human settlements. The problem
is frequently made worse by the widespread use of slash and burn
agricultural techniques. With populations growing at around three
per cent a year and urbanization rates running at roughly double
this, pressure on wood for the rural communities and charcoal for
the towns has increasingly become so great that shortages have
reached critical proportions in several localities, and these
shortages will become more widespread in many countries by the
early 1990s unless significant remedial measures are taken. The
options include biomass conservation by more efficient conversion

to charcoal and better combustion stoves and fuel switching into kerosene or electricity. Reforestation schemes, involving agro-forestry plantations and woodlots are also needed.

While biomass is likely to play a significant role in the energy mix of SADCC countries in the foreseeable future, all of the countries are experiencing some degree of depletion of the standing stock of trees. The situation ranges from cases of severe shortages over substantial portions of the populated rural areas (Lesotho, Malawi, Mozambique, Tanzania and Zimbabwe), to deforestation near urban areas for charcoal supply (Angola and Zambia), to limited local shortages (Botswana and Swaziland).

The depletion of wood stocks is a problem of the first rank, deserving attention commensurate with the stage of deterioration in the particular national context. It is unfortunate that, until recently, little attention was given to this "other energy crisis." Harvesting fuelwood at a rate greater than the sustainable yields of new wood growth depletes the capital of standing stock.

The pace of stock depletion is an accelerating (often exponential) process. The detailed process is quite complex involving demand growth rates, shifting land uses (e.g., clearing for agriculture), regrowth patterns, and the spatial and tenurial accessibility of wood resources to the rural population. The repercussions of wood depletion, or wood shortage, are multiple. It can undermine the physical productivity of the land, through decreased water retention, waterway siltification (with possible decreases in hydropower output), and deterioration of soil quality. Agricultural output could suffer as a consequence. At the same time, the substitution of animal and agricultural residues for increasingly scarce wood resources removes nutrients from the soil cycle and reduces land productivity. The adjustment of household labour budgets to accommodate longer collection times could also undermine agricultural productivity and the rural economy generally. Moreover, the substitution of inferior fuels for wood could be detrimental to rural economic development and quality of life.

Given the potential severity of the ecological, economic, and social repercussions of runaway wood stock depletion, more attention to programmes addressed to ameliorating the problem is indicated. A concerted three-pronged effort will need to be explored in order to: 1) increase the efficiency of end-use and conversion equipment, especially wood and charcoal stoves and charcoal kilns, 2) increase the wood stock through on- and off-farm planting strategies, and 3) substitute abundant and high quality alternatives, e.g., through progressive rural electrification. There is room for considerable action in this area. We discuss possible regional initiatives in Sections 4.F and 5.

4. POLICY ISSUES

In the preceding pages, a sketch of the current energy situation for each of the nine SADCC countries has been provided. Some indication is also given of the likely prospects for future energy provision, taking account of estimated trends in national economic growth, population increase, the urbanization rate, fuel end-use trends, and energy facility project plans. Further, the country-specific analyses have been combined to form a regional picture of evolving requirements for, and supplies of, energy commodities.

On an aggregate physical basis, the regional abundance of modern fuels (electricity, coal, oil) on the one hand, and local insufficiencies of fuelwood, on the other hand, have been underscored. The issue then becomes the role which regional coordination can play in overcoming spatial, financial, and institutional barriers to the cooperative development and utilization of the modern fuels, and in providing a joint framework for mitigating the problems associated with the use of fuelwood.

What are the implications of this synoptic view for the strategic planning of energy futures, both within each country and across the SADCC region as a whole? Clearly, the responsibility for energy planning at the national level rests solely with each government and it is up to each member state, by the judicious deployment of its own resources, to get the best energy bargain it can obtain for itself. Each SADCC country will therefore quite naturally ask itself what special merit there is in the collaborative analysis and planning of energy strategies - how does it help with the purely national problem of adequate and economical energy provision?

4.A Energy Planning: Regional and National

There are a number of ways in which placing energy programme development in a regional framework could help to promote national goals. The first is in identifying those energy-related areas where potential conflicts of interest between states could emerge. It is important to obtain a good assessment of how significant this problem area might become. The second valuable feature of the collaborative approach is that it can highlight opportunities for the interactive and mutually beneficial trade and exchange of energy-related commodities. Further, there are many instances where energy resource boundaries (e.g., fossil fuels, geothermal and hydropower resources, sunshine and wind patterns) run across national boundaries, so that neighbouring countries share a common resource. Under these circumstances, it can often be more effective to share costs of basic data collection and evaluation and, in some cases, of joint resource exploitation. A further merit of the regional approach is that, since matters of national security are often best seen on a regional basis and commonly interface strongly with energy issues, regional energy plans may usefully throw light on issues of national security. Thus, a clear awareness of the regional energy picture, and an understanding of areas of potential inter-governmental collaboration or tension over energy, can help to optimize each national energy strategy.

It must be emphasize that this combined national and regional approach to energy planning is necessarily dynamic, as obtaining a first approximation to crude national energy pictures helps to create a first simple regional picture which can then be used to refine the national pictures into a more conformable set. This in turn, helps to further clarify the regional situation to the benefit of the national energy strategies. This iterative approach embodies a process which should be regarded as a central task of national energy planners within each Ministry of Energy. The materials presented in these documents represent the first step in an optimization process which, it is hoped, will now be carried forward by the energy ministries of the SADCC states.

4.B National Planning

A corollary of the proposition that regional and national energy planning initiatives are best pursued dynamically and interactively, is that national efforts must be upgraded. The main issues have been identified: (1) addressing the problem of wood sufficiency through conservation, supply enhancement, and fuel switching programmes, (2) decreasing the dependence on oil imports through promotion of feasible and cost-effective equipment efficiency improvement actions, substitution with coal and hydropower, and continued exploration for hydrocarbon resources, and (3) identification and diffusion of appropriate renewable energy technologies.

Already a considerable experience has been accumulated at the national level concerning fuel switching programmes, to reduce dependency on oil imports in particular. The experience of Zambia is relevant here. A study was carried out of the industries which consume oil and it was discovered that the twenty largest consumers accounted for 80 per cent of total consumption. This then permitted consultants to be employed to suggest how savings might be made. In Tanzania, there is some inspection by a government instituton to ascertain the least-cost implementation of machinery in particular considering fuel saving.

Zimbabwe has investigated the number of companies using imported fuels, suggesting local fuels to which they could convert. Oil tar, producer gas from coal, electricity and steam from coal are all available locally. To establish consumption figures, the Zimbabwe government first went to the commercial supply firms and obtained a list of 137 companies. Next, each company's fuel needs were examined without raising too much suspicion about why the data was required. A questionnaire was sent out. Data was gathered on process temperatures required and the products made. Following this, a cost exercise was carried out and the findings were that in most cases a significant cost saving will occur. There followed an evaluation of the foreign currency required for switching. This was to satisfy the government that switching would recover the foreign currency within a one year period.

At this stage, the companies were approached for their views and many replied that switching was economically too expensive and technically unfeasible. However, the data supplied convinced many, and these companies then asked for governmental help, to obtain the necessary foreign currency allocation as well as to supply tax relief. The government deemed the former possible but considered the latter unnecessary. In general, however, tax relief is given on capital investment in Zimbabwe. Whilst there is merit for tax relief, it does not make much sense if the companies realise a substantial cost saving. Out of the original 137 firms, a number were allowed to continue with the current use of fuels, because their consumption was not too great. Of the remaining 85, 25 are now changing over, whilst others have asked to delay the switch until the recession abates. When completed, the exercise might save 5 million Zimbabwean dollars.

Zimbabwe is also undertaking conservation measures in agriculture and irrigation. The latter was very expensive in terms of liquid fuels and electricity and the government is encouraging the use of producer gas. On farms, there was a misuse of woodfuel for drying purposes and the use of ethanol and producer gas in farm machinery. Up to 20 per cent of petrol is being replaced with ethanol and some tractors now run wholly on this fuel. This substitution saves up to 20 per cent on foreign currency expenditure. At Hwange, previously the low grade coal was wasted but now power stations are being built on these dumps and, by 1985, it is hoped to generate 1,000 MW of power.

Many countries in the region already have restricted periods when petrol is for sale. In Lesotho, in addition, there are speed limits and punishments for officials using vehicles outside of their work needs. However, there are sometimes limitations on savings that can be made. Lesotho has to subsidise electricity to attract investors given the competition that South Africa poses. A further constraint in several countries are the ties associated

with certain forms of aid. There are also certain structural
limitations to conservation in a less developed country. Current
budget expenditure is frequently easier than larger capital
expenditure. Machinery also has to run longer in an L.D.C. and
multinational capital is generally more competitive than national
firms in the conservation effort. There are constraints as well
as opportunities.

If we turn now to appropriate renewable energy technologies, then
again we find that certain SADCC member states have already built
up a considerable experience in this field. Botswana has found it
useful to categorize RET's (Renewable Energy Technologies) into
three categories:-

Village RET's

Institutional RET's

RET's with commercial and job creation potential.

With the former, there are dangers of the 'missionary approach',
where the vendors of technology push the RET's rather too
aggressively. However, in Botswana, a sequential approach is used
whereby the villagers energy needs are assessed and measured.
Then, in the village meeting place, these assessed needs are
discussed and agreed with the villagers and ways of satisfying
the needs with technological solutions are discussed in depth. If
the villagers agree to try certain RET's, these are constructed
in the rural test villages with villager participation. Currently
there are two in existence, and a third is under selection. In
this manner, RET's, ranging from passively solar cooled and
heated low cost housing and offices in the traditional style,
ovens, evaporative coolers, ice-makers, muscle-powered drilling
machines, lathes, sorghum dehullers and grinders, are all under
consideration.

The institutional technologies mainly centre around health
clinics and centres using water pumping devices (both wind and
solar voltaic) to supply water from Botswana's average borehole
depth of 100 metres, and the provision of passively solar cooled
and heated institutional buildings. Botswana Technology Centre's
HQ, will be the first of the latter in Botswana, and the US
phyicist and architect who designed it, with local inputs, have
just won an international architectural award for its design.
This shows one can have institutional building in the traditional
style with energy savings based on sound science. The country's
water pumping problems are such, that they probably present the
greatest challenge in the developing world. The present solar
pumps work on the photo-electric effect, and presently range from
outputs of five cubic metres to some 15 cubic metres per day from
depths of one to fifteen metres. The given target, however, is 35
cubic metres per day from 100 metres.

Commercially viable RET's, like solar water heaters for rich urban dwellers, are being left to the Botswana private sector. But the country is finding that the market for the electronics needed for solar voltaics must be pioneered by the Botswana Technology Centre. Things like control boxes, chargers and voltage regulators, and solar driven electric cattle fences are well within the country's capability and it has had some success in dissuading its vets from importing such devices through South Africa for their massive cordon fence and movement control programme. Botswana is looking for capital support for its fencer, which it believes to be as good as any in the world and has its own silicon chip high technology electronics. Job creation lies in the introduction of such devices, since even though the components are imported, the soldering and testing of the circuits put onto the 'made-in-Botswana' circuit board, is labour intensive.

Botswana believes it has a RET investment which is well worthwhile, but what is needed is more top-level engineers and financial support for its successful attempts to unpackage high technology RET's which can be made in SADCC countries.

The December 1982 meeting of the SADCC Energy Sector stressed that this area was a particularly fruitful one for regional coordination efforts.

All three areas mentioned at the beginning of this section require policy attention. With regard to the availability of cost-effective technologies to ensure adequate energy supplies, the possibilities are enormous. However, the effective achievement of these goals faces a number of practical and financial hurdles. For example, in order to survive economically and to try to improve GDP growth, SADCC countries must continue to expand their industrial capacity. This often requires oil. The World Bank currently accepts the general guiding principle that if one additional unit of growth requires one extra unit of energy in the industrialized countries, then one unit of growth in Third World countries needs 1.3 units of extra energy to service it. Most oil-consuming processes can be made to run using at least one-third less energy, but this means industrial restructuring, which is difficult and costly. Substitution of hydropower and coal for oil in electricity and process-heat generation can achieve substantial savings of liquid fuels, but is capital intensive to develop. Furthermore, several countries are underexplored as regards oil and gas resources. But prospecting and exploitation are expensive undertakings and, like new dams and mines, of little interest to external multinational capital investment unless there is a real prospect of large surpluses of fuels or power for export sale. Thus, resources adequate only to meet national needs often remain unexploited for

lack of funds, and the recent collapse of the World Bank Energy
Affiliate has dashed earlier hopes of finding new sources of
funding for this.

Solar, wind and geothermal energy resources, biogas and other
renewable sources attracted a great deal of interest in
industrialized countries in the wake of the oil crisis, and most
developing countries were greatly encouraged by this. But
worldwide recessionary tendencies have depressed industry, and
hence current oil demand, so that oil prices began to soften. As
a consequence, the industrialized nations have largely lost
interest in renewable energy, believing that the oil problem can
now be contained by purely fiscal measures. This has meant that
the powerful initiatives which led to the mounting by the U.N. of
the New and Renewables Energy Conference in Nairobi in 1981 have
trickled away, to the dismay of the Third World countries.

Bearing in mind all these constraints on current and future
energy provision, it is therefore all the more important for each
SADCC country to be able to assess accurately its own current and
likely future requirements for various energy commodities in each
consuming sector. Thus, a careful analysis of the quality and
quantity of indigenous energy likely to be available, would allow
the scale of supply effort to be matched to requirements. Limited
economic resources could therefore be allocated more efficiently.
This is the task of energy planning which, if done properly, can
be a powerful tool for prudent development.

But national energy planning covers a broader canvas than the
analysis of national end-use demand and indigenous supply
prospects, important though this role is. In addition, it must be
capable of the detailed planning, and periodic monitoring and
evaluation, of carefully-formulated energy projects. Moreover,
there is an important need to provide a service for screening and
evaluating the wide array of energy technologies (power
generating equipment, industrial process equipment, end-use
appliances, etc.) offered on the world market, so that
cost-effective choices can be made which conform to national
energy objectives. These three tasks require that an energy
planning unit be established, with a mandate to develop an
integrated energy plan, with technically trained personnel having
a wide range of specialities, and with active linkages to
soft-loan facilities for financing national projects. We shall
return to the issue of national energy planning requirements
within SADCC regional contect in Section 5.

4.C Issues in Regional Oil Coordination

The SADCC states, with the exception of Angola, are increasingly
dependent on oil imports as their development proceeds. The oil

price shocks of 1973/74 and 1979 left the oil-importing states paying out up to 75 per cent of their export earnings to keep their transport and industrial sectors operational. This has diminished the capital available for investment, disrupted development plans, and often forced countries to borrow abroad and incur large debt-service burdens.

Purely in terms of indigenous supply, the SADCC region is in a surplus situation for all commercial fuels, including oil. This was discussed in Section 3.D, with quantitative projections of surpluses displayed in Table 15. If ways could be found of redistributing energy in the region, there would be no need to buy any from outside suppliers. This striking finding must surely serve as a tremendous stimulus to future energy cooperation. Furthermore, it immediately highlights the urgency of the need for the SADCC transport policy to take account of energy transport prospects, and therefore the need to develop close cooperation between the SADCC Energy Unit and the SATCC.
An additonal measure for consideration could be the joint purchase of oil in bulk by SADCC member states, which should significantly reduce transport costs.

We shall pose the issues with respect to oil cooperation in the form of a series of eight discussion questions, with additional observations. Clearly, such issues have complex implications and important socio-economic and political management dimensions that can only be responsibly addressed by agreements between the SADCC governments.

Q.1. How feasible is it for SADCC energy interests to join with SADCC transport interests to discuss the problems raised by energy redistribution within the region?

Angola produces enough crude oil to service the projected needs of all states up to 1990, and to still have about 50 per cent of production left over for export outside the region. Beyond 1990, the limit is set by regional refinery capacity and, given construction lead-times, it is not too early to evaluate future refinery needs.

Q.2. Should a detailed study be made of refinery requirements in the region up to the year 2010?

Question 2 above is relevant irrespective of whether future oil supplies come from inside the region or not. If Angola supplies all the oil to the region, this would replace all imports of already refined oils. This means that the refinery capacity in the region has to be doubled anyway. So an important rider to Q.2 is:

Q.3. Is it more economic to build new refinery capacity and import predominantly crude oil or to increase the import of refined products and back out of oil, as far as possible, in favour of coal for thermal electricity and process heat production?

Continuing on the oil refinery theme, it is clear that the existing four functional refineries (Dar es Salaam, Ndola, Maputo and Luanda) together produce a shortfall in middle fractions - diesel/gas oil and kerosene - and an excess of gasoline and residual, relative to the mix of end-use petroleum product demands. Thus, a further supplementary quesion to Q.2. is:

Q.4. Would it be more economic to retrofit cracking capacity to improve the refinery output of middle fractions or to increase the proportion of gasoline engines, via import controls on diesel engines, when replacing old stock?

A further refinery problem relates to the future of the Feruka refinery near Mutare in Zimbabwe, with a capacity of one million tonnes per year but "mothballed" since 1966.

Q.5. Should Feruka be considered as a contributor to future regional refinery capacity, either in its present form or if suitably modified?

A study of Feruka in 1980 found that it would cost US $38 million to reopen it. Even then it would be costly to run, with refinery fuel use and loss running at about 11 per cent of intake. Moreover, it was built to process Iranian light crude, and light crudes are difficult to obtain at present (although Angola's crude tends to be on the light side). Feruka also suffers from a mismatch between the product yield and the market demand for various petroleum fuels. Unless the fraction configuration were changed, the refinery would produce about 50 per cent more gasoline than needed in Zimbabwe initially (though demand for gasoline by 1990 would match output). Although these factors raise questions about the economics of this option, it could cost substantially more to build a new facility, to change the mix of Feruka outputs, or to import additional refined products. A more detailed investigation of the options would be necessary to assess the relative costs. Zimbabwe has commissioned a further petroleum engineering study to examine ways of meeting the country's requirements of refined oil products. Amongst the options being considered are the following. What

should be the role of the Feruka Refinery? Is it better
to continue imports from the spot markets or to go into
joint ventures with the refineries in Mozambique and
Zambia? If Feruka is a viable possibility, should it be
fed with imported Angolan oil?
Currently there is an excess refinery capacity
world-wide, and it may be more economical at least in
the short - and medium-term, for SADCC member states to
import refined products rather than import crude and
refine it locally.

The crucial question determining basic refinery policy is whether
Angola will find it beneficial to export oil to the region. At
the first SADCC Regional Energy Seminar (November/December 1982),
the government of the Peoples Republic of Angola expressed its
willingness to cooperate with all member states in supplying them
with oil and refined oil products. A concrete undertaking has
therefore been made, favourable reciprocal trade agreements also
being made between Angola and other member states over the
purchase of oil. This in term depends upon certain problems being
overcome, such as the different economic systems of the member
states and the best forms of supply to be employed. If ways can
be found to distribute the oil, then, as noted earlier, refinery
capacity for regional self-sufficiency needs to be doubled by the
end of the century (an additional two million tonnes per year by
1990). Under these circumstances problematic issues, like whether
or not to reopen Feruka, may be bypassed in favour of building
new refineries geared to process Angola's crude. Conversely, any
decision to use a mix of crude and refined oils imported from
outside the region, as at present, would place emphasis on
augmenting the capacity of existing refineries as well as
building new ones.

If Angola's oil is used throughout the region, an important
decision is whether to transport crude to the importing states or
to supply refined products direct from Angola. If the former,
there will be less pressure on Angolan refinery potential and
more on refinery capacity in each of the other states. If refined
products are supplied from Angola, transport difficulties
increase considerably while refinery capacity in Angola must
increase rapidly. So the question may be posed:

Q.6. If Angolan oil can be supplied to the SADCC Region, will
it be more economic to transport crude or refined
products, and what implications will this decision have
for transport and for refinery capacity and location?

All the refinery-related issues posed in questions 2-6 above are
affected in a fundamental way by whether or not it will
eventually prove physically possible to distribute Angolan oil

within the SADCC Region. At present, oil imports come in from the
Gulf via Tanzania and Mozambique, or over the Republic of South
Africa's land border with the SADCC states. All countries except
Angola are oil importers and are supplied by these routes.
Angola, apart from supplying its own oil, exports large
quantities by sea, principally to the USA (see Figure 3). Thus:

Q.7. How feasible is it to ship Angolan oil around the Cape
to the existing oil reception ports to supply Tanzania,
Zambia, Zimbabwe, Mozambique and Malawi?

This question involves issues of future relations with
present suppliers in the Gulf and the range of problems
raised by ship transport round the Cape.
Other transport routes should also be examined.
Currently pipelines exist from Dar es Salaam to Ndola
(Zambia) and from Beira to Umtali (Zimbabwe). Even under
existing import arrangements, it is already a matter for
serious discusson whether the Ndola pipeline should be
extended to Harare (Zimbabwe) to transport refinery
products from the somewhat underutilized Indeni
refinery, near Ndola, to Zimbabwe. Additionally, serious
thought is being given to extending the Beira-Umtali
pipeline up to Harare, irrespective of whether the
Feruka refinery is reopened. If both these additional
pipeline extensions were completed, the four countries
of Tanzania, Zambia, Zimbabwe and Mozambique would be
interconnected. Under these hypothetical circumstances,
oil could be transported from Angola and fed into the
pipeline systems, whose existing flows would have to be
reversed. The question is, whether oil could be
transported by rail or even road to Ndola for injection
into the modified pipe system. Or could a trans-Angolan
pipeline be built?

Q.8. What are the costs and benefits of developing a workable
rail or road link, or a pipeline, between Angola and
Zambia to transport Angolan oil, and could this form
part of an integrated oil distribution system utilizing
existing pipelines from Tanzania and Beira?

The above are some of the questions that need further
discussions, as the following general lines of cooperation and
integration are explored:

(1) the establishment of efficient and equitable methods for
the sale of Angolan oil to the other eight countries;

(2) the merits of the various methods of transporting crude
oil and refined products within the region;

(3) the rationalization of refinery capacities, location and product lines;

(4) the harmonization of oil legislation.

4.D Integrated Grid Systems

The enormous hydropower resources in the region, discussed in Section 3.C and 3.D, suggest that electrification could play an important role in development strategies in the area. Indeed, in the absence of an electrification emphasis, the region courts the danger of over-investment in generating capacity, with insufficient demand growth to amortize the large planned expenditures in new facilities.

The deliberative expansion of electricity markets, to replace scarce fuels (oil and biomass) and promote development, appears to be a priority agenda item. Insofar as a transmission grid can be integrated across national boundaries, inexpensive power sources can reach wider markets, demand growth can be accelerated, the problem of costly idle capacity can be avoided, and system reliability can be improved.

Detailed investigation of the opportunities for electricity grid interconnctions is needed. In its absence, the following general observations are offered.

Costs and Benefits of Transmission Systems

Transmission systems reduce supply costs in four ways. First, if regions are interconnected, in the event of generation failure in one region, it is possible to call on the reserves of other regions; in addition, to maintain a given level of system reliability, total reserve capacity with interconnctions is less than that required without interconnections. Second, if peak demands occur at different times in different regions, interconnections permit peak power capacity to be shared, and aggregate peak demand can be met with lower total capacity. Third, if the transmission system is designed to transmit energy in large quantities, power generation in regions rich in inexpensive energy resources can be expanded. This allows other regions to import the cheaper energy, allocating the more expensive forms to the specific uses where they are most appropriate and economical (e.g., oil for transport and coal for industry). In addition, existing generation can be dispatched more economically. With interconnections, larger generation units can be installed, embodying considerable economies of scale.

New high-voltage interconnections, if properly designed, can lead to improved reliability and to system stability. Low-voltage lines in rural regions often tend to grow much longer than was intended, leading to difficulties in maintaining adequate voltage and to frequent power outages caused by loss of synchronization between generation and loads. These problems disappear as more transmission lines and the required substations are installed.

On the other hand, transmisson systems are expensive in foreign exchange terms. Cost estimates for selected elements are given in Table 16; foreign exchange components are, perhaps, 60 per cent for a.c. and 40 per cent for d.c. elements. Many less-developed countries have domestic industries capable of producing wire, towers, transformers, etc., on distribution voltage levels, but lack the technology for the higher voltage levels. The materials, engineering, and production requirements for transmission systems are more exacting. The limited market for transmission systems might make the development of production facilities for these systems unjustified, even on an integrated regional basis.

General Transmission Planning in Southern African States

The location of the major generating facilities with SADCC is, of course, an important consideration. Despite the sometimes vast distances involved in building a regional grid, there are significant opportunities for integration.

The major existing hydro-electric capacity within SADCC is on the Zambezi River system: the Cabora Bassa site in Mozambique (2000 MW), the Kariba South station in Zimbabwe (666 MW), and the Kariba North station in Zambia (600 MW). A further 1000 MW of hydro capacity is located at the large stations at Kafue Gorge and Victoria Falls in Zambia. At some considerable distance is Angola's 287 MW of hydro capacity, located along several rivers in the western part of the country. The largest site at present is 180 MW at Cambambe Dam on the Cuanza River. Other important facilities include 40 MW on the Catumbela River and several other smaller stations. The largest hydro stations supplying the grid in Tanzania are on the Pangani and Kadatu Rivers. Coal capacity within SADCC is concentrated in Zimbabwe (about 900 MW), at Harare, Bulawayo, Umniati and Wankie.

It is noteworthy that the major existing hydro-electric and coal facilities can be circumscribed by a circle of about a 500 km radius. Such a circle includes areas with five SADCC countries -- Zambia, Zimbabwe, Mozambique, Malawi, and Botswana. It also contains agricultural areas and major mining and industrial centres and cities, including Lusaka, Ndola, Kitwe, Maramba, Harare, Bulawayo, Lilongwe, Blantyre, Tete, Beira, and Francistown. This concentration of demand centres, along with the potential for further hydro-development at Kariba, Cabora Bassa, and in Malawi, and the presence of existing grid systems, roads, and railways, creates a promising situation for regional electricity integration.

TABLE 16

<u>SELECTED POWER TRANSMISSION COST ESTIMATES</u>

Facility	Unit Cost (Millions of US $)
500 kV transmission line	$.3 per kilometer
500 kV transmission line	$.4 per kilometer
500 kV substation	$8 each
330 kV transmission line	$.3 per kilometer
330 kV substation	$5 each
220 kV transmission line	$.2 per kilometer
220 kV substation	$4 each
400 kV d.c. transmission line	$.4 per kilometer

Planned new coal-fired capacity (such as at Wankie in Zimbabwe) should be evaluated in the light of a surplus capacity that will exist in this region by 1990. If grid integration were to provide cheaper hydro-electric power where and when it is needed in the region, costly investments in thermal stations could be avoided. Careful consideration of the economic trade-offs between coal and hydropower, in both the national and regional contexts, is called for. In undertaking such evaluations, the capital costs of new coal facilities, the transmission costs for supplying hydropower resources, and the costs, environmental impacts and alternative uses of both coal and hydro resources need to be taken into account.

The first step in transmission planning is the choice of routes and voltage levels for the projected power links. The voltage level for the transmission of a given quantity of power is chosen by compromising between capital costs and the costs of power losses. Whenever possible, lines should follow roads and link up with existing power substations. If transmission facilities already exist, and the required capacity expansion is not too great, existing voltage levels are used to save on costs of new substations.

There are two limitations on the amount of power that can be transmitted for a given power line type: the thermal limit of the line, and its stability limit. In most cases, due to low power-flows and large distances in an interregional power system for Southern Africa, only the stability limits for transmission lines will be important. The stability power limit of a line is the maximum power which can be transmitted to ensure synchronized operation of the system, and depends on the electrical characteristics of operation, transmission, and load. Estimates of this limit can be based solely on the characteristic of the transmission line, if some margin of error is allowed.

As electricity demand levels grow in the Southern African states, stability limits of lines will be approached. More power can be delivered in such a case by installing lines in parallel, by going to a higher voltage level, or by segmenting the overloaded lines with new generation. Temporary relief for the problem can be achieved by the installation of transmission line capacitors or synchronous condensers.

The objectives of an interregional transmission system in Southern Africa would be: to develop a transmission grid system for the Zambia-Zimbabwe-Mozambique hydro-electric complex; to allow power flow to Namibia, Botswana, Tanzania, Malawi, and Swaziland; and to provide peak power support for Tanzania and Malawi. Some of these objectives may be uneconomical to fulfill, considering the relatively small power demands and large

distances. The feasibility of a unified power system for the
Southern African states will depend on the electrification
targets of the participating countries.

Some Hypothetical Projects

The demand for electric power in Botswana to the end of the
century could be readily supplied by a transmission line running
from Bulawayo in Zimbabwe to Gaberone, along or near the railway
to Mafeking. The demand can be met by either a 220 kV double
line, or a single circuit 330 kV line. Assuming that four power
substations would be required (at Francistown, Serowe, Mahalapye,
and Gaborone) and that total right-of-way is 700 kilometers, then
the capital costs for the 220 kV scheme are about US $270
million, and for the 330 kV scheme about US $190 million. This
presumes that a substation, at either 330 kV or 220 kV, with the
required spare capacity already exists at Bulawayo. Although it
is more costly, the double line 220 kV system may be preferrable
for system security and reliability. Botswana has plans for the
development of additional coal-fired electric generation, but the
capital costs for the above transmisson projects are at least
comparable to the investment costs of the coal-fired plant. The
availability of relatively cheap hydro-electric power may render
it uneconomical to build such facilities and burn coal for
electric generation. If hydropower were available the coal could
then be available for such uses as feedstock for nitrogenous
fertilizer production for export and for the satisfaction of
domestic demand, especially in the industrial sector. The
transmission would provide a new market for inexpensive Zimbabwe
electricity, and economically more favourable resource allocation
for Botswana.

Mozambique has large reserves of hydro-electric power. Even if
2000 MW of capacity is put aside for export to South Africa, then
Mozambique's capacity reserve margin (excess of generation over
peak demand) would be over 400 per cent in 1990 and over 100 per
cent in 2000, given existing plans and the load-growth
projections used in this analysis. Mozambique has a
hydro-electric station at Cabora Bassa between Zimbabwe and
Malawi, a station in the north near Tanzania, and one in the
south near Swaziland. A 150 kilometer 220 kV single-circuit link
to Mbabane would cover total demand in Swaziland to the end of
the century, at an investment cost of about US $35 million
(including the cost of substations at each end of the line).
Mozambique could similarly supply power to Tanzania and Zimbabwe
over fairly short transmission lines, to displace the use of
coal-fired generation in these countries. By a judicious choice
of interregional projects, Mozambique could employ otherwise idle
power to help reduce fuel costs (and electric import costs in
Swaziland).

Although the cost of peak power generation appears not to be much of an issue in the study time-frame, the large hydroelectric capacity reserves in Mozambique may also be capable of meeting excess demand during periods of peak-use, when the cost of generation tends to be higher than average. Hydro-electric power is ideal for peak sharing since it not only displaces the use of expensive fuels, but also could make the purchase of special generation facilities unnecessary. Peak power support may be useful in Tanzania, Zimbabwe and Swaziland in 1990, and additionally in Malawi and Namibia by 2000. Transmission schemes to support power sharing are generally less expensive since smaller amounts of power are usually involved. A 220 kV link from Tete to Blantyre (as currently contemplated) would be useful in peak sharing in Malawi, while tying Malawi into Cabora Bassa power. Such a project would cost perhaps US $33 million, exclusive of substation costs. Before extensive considerations can be made about large-scale transmission of peak power, a close look must be taken at the availability of water. It must be decided if there are or will be agricultural constraints on water use, or whether there are physical reasons, such as erosion possibilities or others, that constrain a variable flow of the water.

It appears that the hydro-electric resources of the Zambezi River will play a key role in regional integration. For this reason it would be important to develop a transmission grid that would act as a stable centre for the radial transmission of power to areas like Botswana and Malawi. The nature of a grid system is that each node (or substation) has connections to several other nodes, so that service is readily continued if one or even a few lines suffer an outage. It seems that a Zambia-Zimbabwe-Mozambique grid could be developed using the following as major nodes: Cabora Bassa Hydro, Tete, Harare, Bulawayo, Wankie, Victoria Falls Hydro, Kariba Hydro, and Lusaka. If it is possible to build the grid at the 330 kV level, then presently existing lines in the three concerned nations may be utilized. However, a deeper analysis, which would account for the effects of generation and loads on stability as demand grows, may dictate the use of the 500 kV voltage level for the grid. The order of magnitude of investment costs for a simple 500 kV grid (2500 kilometers of transmission lines and 7 substations) is US $800 or $900 million.

Like Mozambique, Angola has a large surplus of power, amounting to a reserve margin of perhaps 1200 MW in 1990, or even more, depending on construction rates. Depending on the distribution of hydro-electric reserves in Angola, the unused capacity could be tapped by a project transmitting it to Zambia, which could, in turn, export its own displayed hydro capacity. Considering the relatively great power and distances involved, a 400 kV d.c. line would be recommended to deliver the power at Ndola in Zambia.

Investment cost would be somewhere between US $400 to $700 million, depending on routing (this is exclusive of substation capital cost, which might not increase costs by more than 10 per cent). Assuming a project cost of US $600 million for a transmission capacity of 1000 MW,costs would amount to $600/kW. Eventually, Angolan hydroelectric power could also be supplied southward to Namibia.

Summary Comments

The estimates given in the previous sections for a.c. voltage levels are conservative, but the experience is, that once generation and load are taken into acccount in the final stages of planning, changes in previously-estimated voltage levels may have to be made. This is especially true for systems with large amounts of hydrogeneration, which tend to create more than average system stability problems. For this reason utilities are turning to d.c. transmission of hydropower for long distances. There are no stability problems for power which is transmitted by d.c. lines.

Because much of Southern African power is hydroelectric, electricity is inexpensive, so that the economic benefits of interregional transmission systems are great. Although the investment in transmission facilities may become a larger than average fraction of total system costs than in other parts of the world, it may be justifiable in the light of low electricity production costs, and in the interest of avoiding over expansion of regional capacity.

Large investments made now in interregional transmission systems will be further justified if planners keep in mind very long range energy considerations. Reserve margins in each of the countries are at least adequate, given the study results, so that demand will be reliably satisfied on a nation-by-nation base to the end of the century. The issue for interregional transmission planning is economic (better allocation of resources and/or accelerated electrification programmes), and, in the long range, of regional power security. In the very long run, when demand outstrips existing and economically-feasible new hydro resources, if a regionally-integrated transmission system exists, even in elemental form, the precedence, experience, and the infrastructure will be available for the equitable sharing of energy costs and benefits.

4.E Issues in Expanded Coal Use

The large scale increase in anticipated regional coal output has been discussed in Section 3.B. Over 60 per cent of the coal production will be exported, according to the figures in Table

13. The primary regional issues raised by these developments are:
the readiness of the transportation system to handle the
additional heavy trade; the potential for substituting coal for
imported oil; and the need to monitor the environmental
repercussions of increasing coal use.

The railways, largely constructed in the colonial period, were
designed to transport passengers and light trade (e.g.
low-volume, high-value minerals such as gold) to ports. The rails
tend to be of narrow gauge (three feet - six inches), to have
single track, and frequently have steep gradients (up to 2.5 per
cent). Upgrading of the network, principally by improving rail
bed and, perhaps, electrifying, may be required to physically and
economically handle bulk exports such as coal. Additionally, the
upgrading of the main ports, a major concern of SATCC, is a
precondition for the massive increases anticipated in bulk
exports. Export routes for expanded Botswana coal output present
contrasting options: short rail link-ups, with continued reliance
on the South Africa rail system, or construction of a 1000 km
Trans-Kalahari Railway via Namibia to Walvis Bay. The
desirability of coordinating energy planning with transportation
sector initiatives is clear.*

Substitution of regionally produced coal for imported oil could
alleviate foreign exchange burdens in the SADCC countries.
National programmes to encourage coal usage could be beneficial,
to both coal-exporting countries and coal non-exporting countries
in the region. Establishing firm regional markets could: protect
coal-exporting countries from fluctuations in future world coal
demand; promote upgrading of the transportation network; and
provide a basis for beneficial trade reciprocation. Countries
which switch from oil imports on the world market, to increased
coal imports from their neighbours, are likely to enjoy a
substantially less costly fuel, while decreasing foreign exchange
outflows and contributing to overall regional economic
efficiency.

There are four major areas for increased coal usage that come to
mind - power generation, rail transport, thermal usages in
building and industrial processes, and export for foreign
exchange earnings. The first area, the premier coal-switching
option for LDCs dependent on oil-fired generation, is not likely
to be cost-effective in the SADCC region with its abundant,
relatively low-cost hydropower potential. This is especially true
if existing and planned hydropower surpluses can be made

---

* See the companion volume Transport systems in the SADCC Area
for further discussion on the transportation situation.

available through a regional grid system. The second, coal-fired steam engines, may have limited additional potential given relative costs of operation and maintenance burdens. The last two areas (thermal uses and export) provide the backbone of regional efforts to enhance coal utilization. An additional possibility, mentioned earlier, is the use of coal as a feed stock for fertilizer production. Such an option, if proven feasible, could further enhance SADCC regional integration, linking energy, transport and industry to agricultural planning. The harmonization of industrialization, transportation, and coal production plans is the challenge to an integrated approach to regional coal exploitation.

Coal expansion is capital-intensive, costing in the order of US $50 per tonne for annual mining capacity, and infrastructural investments could cost that much again. Foreign investors have, to date, been primarily interested in export markets, where higher financial returns are obtained. One question for discussion, then, is what are the effective strategies for the development of coal to service regional markets? Another question concerns the possibility of using coal as a cooking fuel in the future, to relieve the critical pressure on biomass resources. Is there a viable role for coal as a fuel for cooking that is environmentally satisfactory, low cost, and acceptable to household users?

Several environmental issues are raised by the substantial expansion of coal mining planned in several of the SADCC countries. The planned expansion of coal-fired thermal electricity generation in some of the countries raises additional environmental issues. These issues include: the need for the coal mining industry to maintain its good occupational safety record in the face of expanded activity; the achievement of acceptable water pollution impacts resulting from dust suppression and coal washing; the rational disposal of mine wastes; and the control of air emissions (particularly SO_2) levels in the regional atmosphere that could put forestry, freshwater resource management, agriculture, and human health at risk.

On many of the issues raised above, with respect to coal-switching programmes and increased usage of regional sources, infrastructural requirements for enhanced coal output, consideration of alternative financial and institutional arrangements, research into novel coal applications for the region, and environmental protection, cooperative SADCC efforts would seem opportune.

4.F Traditional Energy Sources

In absolute terms, biomass dominates energy use in the SADCC region. Until recently, many energy planners have presumed that this resource is replenishable and free. Over the next ten years, increasing pressure will be placed upon this biomass resource and, consequently, severe regional shortages will emerge. To lessen the impact of these shortages, there must be a three-fold strategy that seeks to conserve the resource, enhance the supply, and move the population towards the consumption of preferable energy resources. In order to conserve the resource, demand intervention strategies should focus on the establishment of a regional stove design and testing centre, which will provide technical expertise to enable the rapid diffusion of improved urban and rural stoves. Inputs for the various countries on local cooking and consumption patterns would be important in developing efficient stove designs appropriate to local conditions. Climatological considerations may also be significant insofar as heating needs are involved. Additionally, given the probable expansion of charcoal usage in many areas, this centre should have the capability to provide technical assistance on improved pyrolitic conversion methods.

While these demand interventions could in principle halve the current consumption of fuelwood over the next twenty years, difficulties in end-use technology diffusion suggest that the most important area of intervention will probably be supply-enhancement strategies. One difficulty here is that fuelwood is not generally derived from large-scale plantations. The trees for household energy uses come largely from outside the forest. This is also generally true for poles for rural construction purposes. Therefore, there is a need to develop a coordinated supply initiative, based in the agricultural sector, that will place an emphasis on agro-forestry, i.e., the development of trees on individual peasant holdings. As such, it is probable that agricultural extension expertise, rather than forestry expertise, will be needed. Such an effort could help to maintain soil quality while providing energy. Judicious selection of varieties for particular local contexts could also provide additional commodities for rural use.

Forestry expertise can usefully provide technical assistance for village wood-lots and for the establishment of urban shelter belts, which can be used for recreational and environmental management, as well as energy provision. Furthermore, the existing forestry services could be most usefully employed in providing improved management for existing forest resources, especially developing techniques of whole-tree utilization. Attention should also be paid to the increased recovery of agricultural residues on large farms and plantations.

All these supply interventions suggest that, parallel to the conservation effort, there is the need for an institution-building initiative that will, through the agricultural extension service and forestry service, establish a secure energy future for ordinary people.

It is not sufficient, however, that the rural population and the urban core merely maintain their current position. If socio-economic development initiatives are to succeed, they must include a parallel energy development component. Particular attention must be paid in the rural areas to strategies which improve the general standard of living and contribute to agricultural productivity improvement. A regional facility could be available to provide technical help to small-scale users and, where possible, to help them move up the energy ladder towards more versatile forms of traditional fuel utilization, e.g., a producer gas capability for mechanical power and electricity production in the remote areas. This implies further research into the social implications of wood use, and shifts from its use into other fuels.

All the demand and supply-side strategies mentioned are under various stages of consideration and implementation in the SADCC countries. What is required, is the provision of a regional base where this local knowledge and expertise can be gathered, maintained, and disseminated for other members of SADCC. Much more detailed country-case studies are required, in order to obtain the necessary accurate data base on which policy decisions can be made. Detailed national studies can identify specific cultural and socio-economic factors which relate to the collection and use of traditional fuels. A reliable methodology needs to be developed for these field studies. Forest resources are better known than wood resources as a whole, and, as already noted, most people rely on wood gathered from outside the forest areas. While the problem must be addressed primarily on a national, indeed local, basis, due to transport difficulties and local ecological, social, and economic patterns, there is some scope for regional cooperation within SADCC. For example, research and training centres for agroforestry and afforestation schemes, stove/kiln programmes, and demonstration projects, could enhance efforts in this area.

4.G Conservation

The most important emphasis that should exist in the commercial energy sector is conservation (particularly of oil), whenever it is less expensive to save a unit of energy than to deliver an additional unit of energy. To that end, attention should be given to three particular areas, namely:

- A review of existing building codes, and the incorporation into those codes of energy-efficient criteria;

- A review of equipment efficiency, both that manufactured locally and that imported, with a view to establishing regional standards; and

- A review of the possibilities of retrofitting for coal use and efficiency equipment in industrial processes, and shifting to electrification of the rail transport system.

By providing equivalent final service with less energy input, conservation investments are a direct alternative to energy purchases. Vast cost-effective conservation opportunities are known to exist in industrialized countries. The relative benefits in developing countries may be even greater where the alternative, in many cases, additional energy importation, has heavy opportunity costs and foreign exchange penalties.

Programmes for accelerating conservation technology diffusion, once options have been identified, may include a number of different elements: educational/promotional, equipment standards, pricing policies, and financial incentives. While clearly a national emphasis is required here, there may be an important clearing-house role for SADCC in the analysis of conservation options, dissemination of information, and in coordinating conservation programme developments. In addition, a strong case can be made for strengthening and protecting local research institutions in particular patenting energy-saving designs for equipment developed in the region. ESARIPO (English Speaking African Countries International Property Organisation), gives good advice on how to protect inventions through patents and could be used to protect local research initiatives.

5. POSSIBILITIES FOR FURTHER ACTION

The fundamental finding of this exercise is that an optimal
scenario for coordinated regional energy development is likely to
look far different from that which would emerge from a national
focus alone. What appears cost-effective in a limited national
context, may not be the best alternative when reviewed from a
regional perspective. Coordinated planning could move the region
towards greater energy self-sufficiency, avoid duplication of
effort, achieve economies, promote joint initiatives, and channel
scarce development resources toward the areas and sectors of
greatest need.

The questions and issues posed throughout the text so far all
relate to this beneficial interaction between national and
regional energy planning. If the Seminar accepts this important
role for regional energy planning, then it will be logical to ask
what next steps must be taken to develop a practical strategy for
promoting regional collaboration -- exactly what now needs to be
done to set up mechanisms to carry out the necessary work, and
what is the precise nature of this work?

In order to clarify these two questions, it might be useful to
attempt to specify the activities or tasks needing to be carried
out, and then transform these tasks into administrative
functions. The nature of these administrative functions will help
to decide what kinds of institutional arrangements are needed to
service them.

5.A Planning Tasks

When arranging for energy provision, the following activities,
both at national and regional levels, are necessary:

1. National Demand Assessment

    Collect data on the range of end-use requirements in
    each country, and estimate what type and quantity of
    energy is currently needed in each demand category.
    Develop scenario projections of demand evolution, based
    on "business-as-usual" demographic, economic, and
    behavioural patterns. (The analyses carried out here
    mark a beginning of this process.)

2. Estimate Degree of National Demand Flexibility

    Outline in broad qualitative terms the levels of
    flexibility in these end-use demand patterns: e.g. (1)
    specify practicable conservation opportunities wherever

these exist (e.g. energy savings by redesign of new buildings; improved energy conversion and end-use efficiency; possibilities for fuel-substitution etc. These prospects have then to be transformed into practicable institutional arrangements and administrative functions.

3. Assess Energy Supply Prospects

    Specify the range and amounts of each of the indigenous energy sources available within each country, and the realistic prospects for getting these on stream in the short (0-5 years) and long-term. Estimate the future prospects for the continued supply of imported fuels and their likely costs.

4. Compare National Demand Needs With Estimated Supply Potential

    Try to match national demand (1 above) with national supply (3 above), and see how far the degree of flexibility found within the demand pattern (2 above) can be used to economically accommodate demand to supply.

5. Collate National Demand/Supply Information to Obtain a SADCC Regional Picture

    Examine what is known about the regional supply/demand picture as a whole and pinpoint where there might be some potential supply surpluses in other countries. Study their use potential.

6. Evaluate Costs and Benefits of Regional Collaboration on Supply Provision

    Investigate what kind of benefits would accrue from inter-governmental cooperative development of, for instance: jointly-organized hydropower potential; integrated grid systems; joint inter-state transport facilities for coal and oil; shared prospecting arrangements for fossil fuels and geothermal potential, etc. If the benefits appear to be considerable, estimate costs, manpower and other efforts needed to achieve shared exploitation.

7. Assess the Impact of Collaboration on the National Energy Situation

Examine how the new (more plentiful and/or less costly) energy facilities, thus developed under regional collaboration, could benefit the national supply pictures.

8. Develop a Set of National and Regional Energy Policy Proposals

In the light of 1-7 above, formulate a clear-cut set of policy proposals within each national energy plan developed in response to the information emerging from 1-7 above.

9. Transform Policy Proposals Into Projects

Development of concrete plans for specific projects which will put the proposals into action. Some of these projects will be aimed at the national level, and will be solely the responsibility of each individual country to implement. Others will involve regional collaboration through SADCC.

10. Financial Implications

Plan the levels of finance required to mount each project and formulate ways of obtaining this. Here again, some financial planning will be referable to national and some to regional projects.

11. Research and Development Requirements

Formulate what types of associated R&D are needed to promote the above list. So far, this list involves energy planning expertise, computerized information management facilities and high-level technical capability. A further item to be included here is the need for a group of expert personnel to carefully screen the performance characteristics of imported energy technology under local conditions. This applies principally to the national energy pictures but the capability could be mounted on a shared (regional) basis.

12. Manpower and Training Needs

Lastly it is important to estimate what kind of technical manpower and external expert support services will be required to mount 1-11 above, and what types and levels of training are involved to sustain it in the long term.

Further elaboration of these activities are presented in the
subsections below.

5.B National Energy Assessment

The first four tasks itemized above, involve the collection and
systematization of energy use data, and the development of
projections of future supply and demand configurations. An
integrated analysis of the country's energy needs and resources
over time provides a roadmap for assessing policy options.

There is a need to review the individual, national planning
mechanisms for each of the SADCC member countries. At present, it
is not possible to accurately determine whether, in fact, the
energy plans and projects of individual member states are
cost-effective in terms of overall SADCC requirements and
opportunities. Conversely, what is cost-effective in SADCC terms
might not be considered so by individual member states. Until the
national planning efforts are integrated with the overall SADCC
efforts - ideally by the adoption of common criteria and
energy-information systems - the identification, and appraisal,
of individual projects is hampered.

A computerized planning system can be a very useful aid in the
national energy-assessment process. A properly designed system
fulfills three major functions: (1) it serves as an information
bank and guide to data development and synthesis, (2) it provides
long-term projections of supply/demand configurations, and (3) it
computes the impacts of user-selected policy and technology
initiatives, with respect to near and long-term supply and demand
balance, capital requirements, costs and benefits, and foreign
exchange accounts.

Elements of such a system were employed in the preliminary
national assessments produced for this investigation. The output
summaries collected in the Annex represent a prototype of the
kinds of background assessments suggested here (the land-use,
demographic, project cost/benefit, and biomass resource modules
of the LEAP System were not used in the current exercise).

Considerably greater detail could be usefully obtained than that
reflected, for example, in Output Table 2, the breakdown of
end-use consumption. For instance, the energy contents of
imported and exported goods, including food, could be assessed.
An example of how energy demand data could be collected, is laid
out in Table 17. In practice, even more detail is desirable
(e.g., breakdown of household sector by income class, industry by
product category, agriculture by end-use). The task of completing
such a table is less formidable than it appears at first sight,
because many of the combinations of fuel-type and end-use (a

TABLE 17

SAMPLE END-USE DATA FORMAT

		MOBILE (TRANSPORTABLE) ENERGY SOURCES																							STATIONARY ENERGY SOURCES								
		GASEOUS FUELS					LIQUID FUELS							SOLID FUELS								BIOENERGY				GEO-THERMAL		SOLAR		HYDROPOWER				AIR
		BIOMASS		MINERAL			BIOMASS			MINERAL				BIOMASS				MINERAL COALS				MUSCLE POWER								LAKE		SEA		
		1	2	3	4	5	6	7	8	9	10	11	12	13	14	15	16	17	18	19	20	21	22	23	24	25	26	27	28	29	30	31	32
SECTOR	END-USE	Biogas	Wood Gas	Liq.Petrol Gas	Natural Gas	Coal Gas	Ethanol	Methanol	Vegetable Oils	Gasoline	Kerosenes	Gasoils	Residual	Charcoal	Crop Wastes	Dung	Wood	Cooking	Steam	Other	Nuclear	Animal	Human	Electricity	Hot Rock	Steam	Photovoltaic	Thermal	Macrohydro	Minihydro	Ocean Thermal	Tide/Wave	Wind
...AL ...SEHOLD	Cooking / Hot Water / Space Heat / Light / Cooling & Power																																
...AN ...SEHOLD	Cooking / Hot Water / Space Heat / Light / Cooling & Power																																
...IC. ...ON.	Traction on Farm / Plant & Harvest / Irrigation																																
...ISTRY ...E	Space Heat / Light / Process Heat / Cooling & Power																																
...US.RY ...L ...AN (FORMAL)	Space Heat / Light / Process Heat / Cooling & Power																																
...USTRY ...LL ...AL (INFORMAL)	Space Heat / Light / Process Heat / Cooling & Power																																
...OOLS & ...PITALS ...'T. ...LDINGS	Cooking / Space Heat / Light / Cooling & Power																																
...ICES	Cooking / Space Heating / Light / Cooling & Power																																
...ELS	Cooking / Space Heat / Light / Cooling & Power																																
...NSPORT	Road-Private / Road-Non-Priv. / Rail / Air / Other																																
...CTRICIT																																	
...D GAS																																	
...RCOAL																																	

total of 1312 cells in the sample table) are not applicable, e.g., Animal Muscle Power applies only to Agricultural Production and Road Transport. Note that electricity, wood-gas and charcoal, as well as being placed as fuel sources, are also listed at the foot of the end-use demand column. This is simply a convenience device to clarify exactly how much wood is needed to make charcoal and wood-gas and how much gas, oil, nuclear, hydropower, etc., is needed to produce electricity.

The systematic (preferably computerized) collection of data for each of the valid cells of the table is the primary task of the "National Energy Planning Unit" in each country. The completed table provides the basic data for national planning. In using it as a guide to policy, each valid cell can be augmented in several important ways.

Each valid cell of the table shows the estimate of "Actual Energy Demand" for a particular fuel-type under a particular end-use. This demand is, of necessity, equal to "Actual Energy Supplied"; otherwise it would not exist. However, from a careful consideration of the prevailing domestic, commercial and industrial sector characteristics, it is possible to obtain a reasonable estimate of the existence of potential demand which remains unmet. This demand would only be expressed if the appropriate fuel supply were readily available and/or less expensive. Many tropical villages rely on firelight for illumination after dark, but would readily switch to electric light or kerosene lamps if these were available. This "Additional Desired Demand" (for each end-use) is mirrored by an "Additional Potential Supply" (for each fuel type) which, although often physically available, remains underplayed for a variety of reasons. It is a rather common situation in many developing countries for financial, technological or organizational hurdles to prevent the bringing on stream of potentially important energy supply sources. Furthermore, existing capacity (e.g., hydro-facilities, coal mines) may be under-utilized and be a potential source of additional supplies.

A knowledge of two further statistics is vital to the energy planner. The first indicates the potential for energy saving on the demand side by: improving end-use efficiency with better wood or charcoal stoves, more efficiently maintained internal-combustion engines, buildings designed to minimize cooling or heating needs etc.. This "Demand Conservation Potential" has its counterpart in a "Supply Conservation Potential", which indicates how energy supply can be made to go further e.g. via improved conversion efficiencies for electricity from diesel, or charcoal from wood.

A final important statistic is how far it is possible to replace one type with another e.g. wood for cooking by coal, kerosene or electricity.

All these figures taken together can yield a "Demand Target" for a particular end-use and fuel-type, as well as a "Supply Target" for a particular fuel type. This task can be completed from existing or collectible statistics in energy units (e.g., GJ) for a base year (say 1980). A second table can be projected from the most likely estimates of relevant statistics for, say, 1990, and so on. It is also possible to use these tables as a framework for costing energy. Thus, alternative configurations can be compared economically, providing a guide to programme and policy development. The above description is illustrative of the kind of work that could be done by the National Energy Planning Units under Tasks 2, 3 & 4 above.

5.C Regional Assessment of Combined National Energy

The data and analysis developed for each country under Tasks 1-4 above, could be transmitted by the national energy planners for collation into a Regional Energy Picture by a SADCC "Regional Energy Planning Group." This is Task 5 and gives a regional demand/supply picture. The Regional Energy Planning Group would also consult with National Planners, to assess whether it would be worthwhile to redistribute any national energy supply surpluses (recognized under "Additional Potential Supply"). By scrutinizing primary potential on a regional basis, the Regional Energy Planning Group would also be in a position to evaluate whether certain collaborative projects would be ultimately beneficial at the national level.

As an illustration of this, one could pose a hypothetical scenario for the collaborative use of Angolan oil, which could be rigorously analysed by the Regional Energy Group, with a view to establishing a prima facie case for a project:

Step 1   Angola considers reducing its planned refinery-building programme, to a level sufficient to cover its own requirements only.

Step 2   Angola uses the money saved to organize the shipment of crude oil to Beira and Dar es Salaam.

Step 3   Some of the crude landed at Dar es Salaam is refined for use in Tanzania, and the rest is piped direct to Ndola where it is refined for Zambia's use.

Step 4   All the crude at Maputo is refined. Some is maintained for use by Mozambique and the rest is piped to Feruka for use by Zimbabwe.

(Separate arrangements are made for Malawi).

Step 5   During the time these actions are being
          established, a new modern refinery is built at
          Feruka, or the existing refinery is upgraded and
          made operational, and, subsequently, the
          Beira-Feruka pipeline is modified to deliver crude
          oil again (non-refined products) to the new
          refinery.

Step 6   A new pipeline is built from Feruka to Harare to
          deliver the refined products from the new Feruka
          refinery.

Step 7   Careful consideration is given to building
          substantial and secure storage capacity for
          combined oil at Dar es Salaam, Beira, Ndola and
          Feruka, to act as supply reservoirs if, for any
          reason, shipped or piped supplies of crude are
          unavoidably interrupted.

Several other oil scenarios, collaborative electrical grid
scenarios or other joint regional projects, could be examined in
this way. For example, with respect to electricity, there is the
need for consideration of a consolidated regional electricity
generation strategy. Such a strategy would require a study of the
cost-effectiveness of a SADCC electrical grid system, and the
development of appropriate criteria for rural electrification,
where the impact on the quality of life is so great that
conventional costing methodology may have to be abandoned. In
addition to the need for a major review of regional oil-use
possibilities (one hypothetical scenario was presented above),
attention must be paid to the design of fiscal instruments which
would ensure that, if Angola became the major oil supplier to
SADCC, supply could be guaranteed and a just pricing policy, both
to the supplier and to the end user, maintained. In a regional
strategic sense, there is also need to consider the possibility
of pipeline and/or railway extensions linking the eastern part of
the SADCC region, where most supplies are currently landed, to
the western part. There is also the need for an examination of
the coal prospects of southern Africa; in particular, an attempt
should be made to determine if an integrated export strategy for
coal from the SADCC region is possible. Within SADCC, there is
the need for a critical examination of which industrial processes
could be best served by coal as an energy source, as well as
examining the possibility of the accelerated utilization of coal
in households.

The foregoing describes, in essence, the work of Tasks 6 and 7.
Such analyses would for the basis for discussion between the

Regional Energy Planning Group and the Naional Energy Planning Units from each country, and are designed to influence the formulation of each national energy plan, as well as to help design the agreed collaborative regional proposals (Task 8). Both national and regional groups would then be able to transform these Planning Proposals into proposed projects to put on the ground (both National Projects and Regional Projects - Task 9).

5.D Regional Energy Projects

Each proposed Regional Project would require a great deal of development work to plan, to secure adequate financing and to start up. It may be worth considering whether this heavy burden could be shared more equitably, by arranging for different SADCC states to take responsibility for developing different proposed Regional Projects, under the overall co-ordination of the SADCC Energy Group.

The following (are suggestions of) possible regional projects for further study and evaluation:

1. Regional collaborative development of hydropower potential.

2. Regional collaborative development of an integrated electricity-transmission grid system.

3. Co-operation on the building of a SADCC oil-pipeline network.

4. Regional planning of data-collection for sunshine, wind and hydropower potential.

5. Joint organization for the management of prospecting arrangements for fossil fuels and geothermal potential.

6. Regional Centre(s) for energy R & D, training and energy information management.

7. A regional advisory group for legal, economic and environmental arrangements needed when negotiating contracts for energy-related activities between SADCC states and multinational industries (e.g. coal extraction contracts).

Much of the rationale for the first five points above, is already included, either in the country studies or earlier in this document. Perhaps it is worthwhile at this point to expand a little on the utility to SADCC of points 6 and 7 above.

5.E. Regional Centre(s)

Sound future energy provision, both at national and regional
levels, is built upon the professional knowledge of personnel
with a wide range of expert technical capacity, backed up by the
institutional capacity to carry out the following:

1. Assemble the data base for the national energy plan, and
    continue to update and collate energy data collected in
    an orderly (computerized) format.

2. Evaluate national energy data sets, in order to
    formulate optimal, cost-effective policy proposals and
    develop carefully-costed energy projects.

3. Review the technical suitability of "energy hardware"
    and other energy-related technology most appropriate to
    the socio-economic and cultural milieu of the country
    concerned.

4. Develop techniques for the establishment and maintenance
    of fuelwood tree-planting programmes, via agroforestry
    and other types of afforestation designed to mitigate
    fuelwood shortages.

5. Train forestry/agriculture extension-service workers, to
    liase with the rural population to promote 4 above, and
    to diffuse knowledge of improved wood stoves, etc.

6. Develop a seeds centre for collection, storage and
    distribution of fuelwood-tree seeds (linked to 4 and 5
    above).

7. Develop capacity to formulate/monitor progress and
    evaluate success of energy related projects.

8. Develop standards, procedural guidelines and codes of
    practice, for the management of energy provision and
    energy-related projects in the SADCC Region.

9. Develop economic and legislative expertise in
    negotiating projects with external participants -
    aid-agencies, multinational companies, etc.

10. Maintain a reference collection of energy related data
    for the SADDC Region as well as an up-to-date energy and
    development library.

Careful consideration should be given to how fulfillment of these
vital tasks, for one or more special Regional Centres under the
auspices of a Regional Energy Planning Group, can be best
achieved in the SADCC context.

5.F Planning Procedures

SADCC countries are currently in a uniquely fortunate position to co-ordinate, harmonize and standardize energy management procedures - a situation which might never occur again. And so the opportunity must be grasped now.

The administrative flows, for the foregoing discussion of combined national and regional planning and project development, may be conveniently summarized in Figure 5. The SADCC Energy Group (Angola) would naturally be responsible for co-ordination of all regional operations, and in particular for setting up the Regional Energy Planning Group (REPG) whose members would include representatives from each SADCC state.

Careful consideration should be given to the idea of appointing a UNDP-supported Energy Planning Advisor to each National Energy Planning Unit. This procedure has proved very successful in the past in several African countries.

The National Energy Planning Unit focused in the country's Ministry of Energy (or cognate ministry), develops the energy data base and analysis as described above, and consults with the REPG on its national data, so that the REPG can inject a sense of the Regional context into the National Planning Unit during the phase when it is developing the National Energy Plan. Out of this will come National Projects more carefully attuned to the Regional Energy context.

The Regional Energy Planning Group, after synthesising the national energy data sets, would develop Regional Energy Policy proposals, with technical support from the regional centres, which will be discussed with individual countries via their National Energy Planning Units. Each proposal (along the lines indicated in Subsection 5.D) may be of special interest to the country which helped to develop it with the Regional Energy Planning Group. In such cases, the country concerned may wish to take responsibility for promoting it under the overall co-ordination of the SADCC Energy Group (Angola) and, after inputs from external consultants, transform it into a concrete Regional Energy Project which is put up to the SADCC Energy Group for endorsement, prior to execution.

Figure 5

FLOW-DIAGRAM FOR PROPOSED DEVELOPMENT OF
NATIONAL AND REGIONAL ENERGY PROJECTS

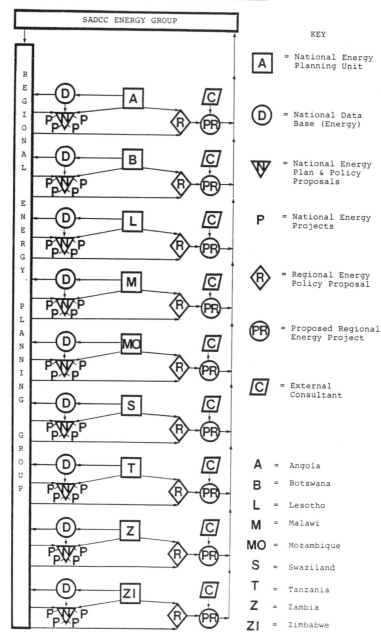

CONCLUSIONS OF THE CONFERENCE

Energy Data Base

Throughout the Seminar, there was a general concern about the need for a better regional data base for energy and energy related items, (e.g. land use, energy costs) computerised in a conformable manner over the whole SADCC region, usable as a regional energy planning tool and accessible to all Member States. The LEAP (LDC Energy Alternative Planning) system developed by the Beijer Institute and the Energy Systems Research Group and used for all energy data management throughout this Seminar received support as the appropriate system.

Energy Related Legislation And Institutional Arrangements

Concern was expressed that the current legal and institutional structures available to each Member State to handle energy related issues were incompatible and urgently in need of harmonisation. A careful study and analysis should be made of potential mismatches with a view to obtaining a regionally compatible legal/institutional system for energy management.

Rural Household Demand Supply

Traditional fuels (mainly fuelwood and charcoal) used for cooking, water and space heating and lighting in the rural sector account for 52 - 94 per cent of the total energy consumption of SADCC States. The Seminar concluded that it would not be realistic to move away from the use of wood for the foreseeable future. It was further agreed that, because of heavy consumption, woodfuels were becoming scare to a point where serious deficits have already occurred in many Member States. Several actions designed to improve supply and efficiency of use should be implemented, as indicated below.

SADCC Member States were urged to carry out (using a common methodology) comprehensive field surveys in sufficient detail to elucidate fuelwood demand/supply (current states and future trends) in relation to population distribution. Such national data, when obtained would also be communicated to the regional energy data resource of which it would form an integral part.

Woodfuel Supplies

The Seminar clearly understood the above needs as fundamental to the maintenance and efficient use of woodfuel stocks. Likewise, it was equally understood that to be of optimal use, wood fuels have to be readily available close to human settlements. This means trees <u>outside</u> the forest areas. And moreover these fuelwood trees have <u>to grow</u> in such a manner that they do not compete with essential food production. Where villages exist and where good rain-fed agricultural land is not at a premium, woodlots may be appropriate. Where such conditions do not occur, modern methods of growing trees side by side with food crops to the benefit of both (agro-forestry and sylvi-agriculture) are now to hand and rapidly being expanded. What is needed now is the development of Rural Energy Centres where these fairly simple techniques can be learned by villages and small farmers. At the same time, such Centres would be able to act as focal points, disseminating knowledge on which tree species to grow, how to identify and collect seed from them in the wild, how to plant, transplant and care for the growing seedling trees. The Centres could also provide information on efficient wood-stove design and any other new/renewable energy innovations as they become practicable. Since women play such an important role in agriculture, woodfuel gathering and cooking, there is considerable merit in involving women as the energy advisers at such Centres.

Energy And Rural Development

The Seminar paid special attention to energy needs on the farm, for the farming family and for the rural community (schools, clinics etc.). It was recognised that adequate energy in the right form added immensely to the quality of life of the rural population. Whilst it was clear that energy planning at the national level if properly carried out and implemented would automatically provide many of the answers to a large number of pressing issues in this area (especially rural electrification) certain interesting problems stood out as meriting attention.

Solar photovoltaic collectors, although still very expensive, may in certain cases (electric fencing, telecommunications and water pumping in remote areas) merit the extra investment. Their unique relevance should be explored. Another interesting potential development is the possible use of the mineral Zedite for solar energy collection. Proven deposits exist in Botswana and exploration for this mineral should be encouraged elsewhere in the region.

Industrial And Commercial Energy

These activities account for about a quarter of the energy used in the region as a whole, with large scale industry consuming just under half of this amount. Carefully carried out energy demand analyses performed as part of the data gathering needed for national energy planning can usually pinpoint the more important inefficiencies of usage or opportunities for fuel switching to more plentiful but neglected or indigenous energy sources e.g. oil tars, producer gas from coal, or coal for steam and electricity ("energy alternatives"). Often what is needed to start the change is a stimulus to do this being given to the company concerned.

Delegations at the Seminar provided a wealth of experience in ways of doing this from tax incentives for fuel switching to actual demonstrations being given to a company that large sums of money could actually be saved by deploying "energy alternatives". These experiences should be collected and carefully documented in the form of a Comparative Regional Review to encourage their emulation elsewhere. This is the essence of good national energy planning.

Regional Transport Systems

Because of its oil-derived fuel basis, transport is the largest single consumer of imported oil (up to 70 per cent in some instances) and the heaviest drain on foreign exchange earnings (usually 25 - 50 per cent across the SADCC oil importing region). With the expected rise in trade in the coming decades the pressure on the transport systems of the region will become very great. The Seminar had already noted that as a region, SADCC was most likely to be in energy balance or surplus for oil, coal and hydropower up until 1990. This encouraging news was offset by the fact that most of these primary energy sources are to be found only at great distances from their points of maximal utilisation. Thus, although "energy for transport" is a vital issue, the "transport of energy" is even more important. This raises the issue of the interface between SATCC and the SADCC Energy Sector in an acute form. It was clear that the Seminar felt how important it was to inject this energy dimension into the transportation planning of SATCC. It should be able to indicate the level of energy saved in relation to capital and recurrent costs on the upgrading of railways and roads. Additionally, the role of SATCC in optimising transport networks to maximise energy saving and security considerations, on both energy carrying traffic and on other forms of transport, was very great.

Oil

The Angolan Delegation indicated that the People's Republic of Angola was ready to seek economically appropriate ways of marketing their oil products within the SADCC region. This information was welcomed by all delegations and unanimously noted with approval.

Various possibilities for the intra-SADCC marketing of Angolan oil were then considered including:

1. The creation of a SADCC common oil policy as an attempt to
    stabilise oil prices and revenues within the SADCC region for
    the next 10 years.

2. The upgrading and/or building of SADCC national refinery
    capability to process Angolan crude, versus the importation
    of refined products to the SADCC States.

These and similar considerations were already included in a
special study requested as a matter of priority 20-23 July 1982,
by the SADCC Council of Ministers (on how the SADCC countries
might achieve self sufficiency in the supply of oil products).

Electricity

The Seminar noted that as a unitary region SADCC was in surplus
of required hydroelectric power up until 1990 and beyond. Many
questions relating to the stepwise creation of a regional
electricity grid system were discussed. In particular the problem
was raised as to what level of excess capacity was reasonable
bearing in mind the investment cost of undertaking this versus
the opportunity costs of other (non-energy) investments.

New And Renewable Energy Technologies

It was recognised that the resources of the SADCC countries
should be pooled in order to take advantage of the collective
expertise of scientific skills and funds and to avoid wasteful
overlaps. The Seminar agreed to investigate the possibilities of
setting up a regional centre on Renewable Energy Technologies
(RETs) with emphasis on approaches to forestry and agro-forestry.
The purpose of this centre might be to:

(a) Serve as an information clearing house on RETS research
    and development regionally, on social and economic
    considerations in RETS adoption, and on the practical
    experiences in the various countries.

(b) Provide research, development and demonstration on all
    relevant aspects of RETs. Attention would be paid to the
    possibility of recovering "retarded" technologies (those
    that virtually disappeared in the era of inexpensive
    oil) and, in particular, the prospects for regional
    production of all or components of RETs. SADCC can and
    should begin a programme aimed at "unpackaging" RETs in
    order to become capable of producing appropriate RETs
    components regionally.

(c) Study the possibilities of creating mechanisms for
    linking national centres and nationally-based

researchers with one another in order to produce a regional network of energy research and a clearing house for energy information.

Coal

The Seminar noted that a large scale increase in the level of coal production is anticipated in the 1980s with the bulk earmarked for export to world markets. The main issues connected with expanded coal production are the adequacy of the transport system, the potential for increased regional use (e.g. fuel switching or coal stoves) and environmentally sound mining and usage.

SPEECH BY THE MINISTER OF ENERGY AND PETROLEUM OF THE
PEOPLE'S REPUBLIC OF ANGOLA AT THE CLOSE OF
THE SADCC ENERGY SEMINAR.

Harare, 3rd December 1982.

I would like, firstly, as Minister of Energy and Petroleum of the People's Republic of Angola, the coordinating state of the energy sector of SADCC, to thank the Government of Zimbabwe, and in particular, the Ministry of Industry and Energy Development through their distinguished Minister, for his kindness in acting as host and for his tireless efforts towards the success of this Seminar which has now reached its close; and for the untiring effort and great dynamism shown by the Government of Zimbabwe through its Ministry which Your Excellency leads, the extreme competence, clarity and technical knowledge of the consultants entrusted by your Ministry to give technical assistance on all important matters, as well as the prompt and understanding help given to this event by other Public Sectors of your country. Comrade Minister we are extremely touched, and positively convinced that Angola can depend on a united effort and understanding from all the member countries of SADCC for a continually growing development in coordinating cooperation in the Regional Energy Sector.

This seminar took place at a time of extreme importance in the life of our region, in the political and in the military field. We face various diversionary manoeuvres, threats and acts of military invasions from the racist South African Regime.

In Angola, our valiant armed forces daily confront the powerful South African army on our border with Namibia.

The explosion of mortars, the movement of tanks, air combat, the launching of troops, the destruction of means of communication and other important social and economic objectives constitute a sad and fearsome scene in a country which only wishes peace and progress. The Angolans fought for their independence in search of a better more peaceful and civilized life, and they have continued their fight for the last seven years.

Our enemies do not desire our happiness and well being, they do not wish our progress and liberty. They want to see us divided and weak, subjected to their pressures and demands, without our own personality and sense of life. Our personality and our pride in being free is an open sore on their chests. To the efforts of Mozambique in carrying out a great number of projects of regional impact with a direct and indirect benefit to other SADCC countries, in the field of transport and communications, our enemies retaliated by sending special troops of their regular army or with threats of invasion on a large scale.

The support to South African democrats and the legitimate humanitarian assistance to the refugee victims of the most inhuman and cruel racism that history has known since the Second World War, is used as nothing but a gratuitous pretext for South Africa to carry out destabilizing policies and sabotage actions to undermine the direction of development that Mozambique has undertaken.

But Mozambique and Angola are not the only victims. Threats, sabotage and open aggression are equally carried out against our brother countries of Zambia, Botswana and Zimbabwe and against the Kingdom of Lesotho.

The racist South Africans and their allies are fearful of the results of our unity and our coordinating cooperation in the SADCC framework.This fear has acquired proportions of complete despair, motivated by our gradual but secure progress.

More than ever, it is time for union and mutual solidarity to be materialized in economic, political, scientific and technical cooperation.

At a time in which African unity takes concrete steps in order to maintain its cohesion, SADCC must search for a greater unity and strength of mind.

We are sure that in the very near future we shall have in our midst a free and independent Namibia so that we may become stronger and more sure of ourselves.

Excellencies, ladies and gentlemen. At the last session, tomorrow, of the sub-committee of energy officials, we will be in a position to look towards the coming years with the knowledge of the immense work carried out in 1982. For the first time, the SADCC energy sector will present at the donor's annual conference some projects of regional impact, while all the necessary basic technical work continues to be developed to March 1983.

Since February 1982, two meetings have taken place at Ministerial level, four at the level of officials, and one regional technical seminar within the Energy Sector. With the approval of the Counsel of Ministers, Angola has started, as a "matter of priority", the study of HOW THE MEMBER STATES OF SADCC CAN ATTAIN SELF-SUFFICIENCY IN THE AREA OF THE SUPPLY OF OIL PRODUCTS and with the support of various Governments, such as Belgium, Norway, the United Kingdom, Brazil and Italy and with a substantial support from the European Economic Community, Angola continues to establish the technical and administrative unit which has the task of supporting the SADCC member states, in the implementation of the regional energy programme.

The activity of this technical and administrative unit is already directed at various aspects of cooperation, such as the negotiations that brought about the intention to finance the project in the domain of electricity between Mozambique and Zimbabwe, the second part of the survey for self sufficiency in the area of supply of oil products and of a regional seminar on wood fuels and its byproducts, to be held in the middle of next year.

Negotiations are continuing for the financing of the Centre for Regional Training in Petroleum, with positive results.

Another outstanding result of our activity during the year that is now ending, was the adoption in September, by the SADCC energy Ministers, of the criteria for evaluation of projects with a regional character. This document must be our principal guide in the selection and evaluation of projects, and the ideas for projects, in our sector.

Our legitimate right and duty in seeking economic, technical and scientific development and the well-being of our people through the realization and implementation of new projects must continue to take into account our strategy, and discipline, conscientiously conceived and approved.

I solemnly present these points for reflection at the conclusion of the first regional energy seminar.

Excellencies, ladies and gentlemen.

In April of 1983 the energy Ministers will meet to select and approve a list of projects of regional impact as a result of a preparatory study carried out by Angola with the support of Belgium. The report which will be presented by Angola will not fail to take into account the recommendations of the present Seminar, as well as the results of the preparatory studies already carried out.

As Minister of Energy and Petroleum of the coordinator state of the energy sector, I positively share the preoccupations expressed by the Minister of Industry and Energy Development of the Republic of Zimbabwe at the inauguration of this important event.

It is a fact that the region needs progress, needs to attain its objectives of economic and technological development and social well being with a politically coherent attitude, with the realization and implementation of projects which from today and not tomorrow, meet our strategic and tactical objectives in the framework of coordinated regional cooperation.

The studies presently underway, together with the recommendations of the present seminar, will give us the possibility of critically and impartially deciding in April on the projects of primary interest and suitability for the region.

Excellencies, Ladies and Gentlemen.

The coordination of the SADCC energy sector is conscient of the problems of the region. Our regional perspective and the zeal in obtaining the best results of a coordinated regional cooperation particularly aim to complement the national efforts for development, progress and well being.

We believe that the session is fully conscious that a coordinated regional cooperation within the framework of SADCC, aims primarily to complement the national efforts and further rationalize the utilization of both human and material resources and to achieve a degree of technical and economic complementarity, based on reciprocal advantage.

SADCC emerged, and is continually strengthened, on a basis of equality and respect among the states, in its honesty of relations and principles to benefit the region, to make the member states technically and economically stronger and to establish the necessary mechanisms for a secure progress.

The Peoples Republic of Angola is favourable to the principle of sharing with the states of the region its petroleum resources on the basis estimated by the results of the surveys presently underway and with the principle of reciprocity of commercial advantages. In the same way that was considered during the course of this seminar, this objective must continue to deserve a profound analysis according to our political will.

Different economic, technical and commercial options must necessarily be faced. In any case, the region must remain aware that it seeks in fact, real and global self sufficiency.

Excellencies, ladies and gentlemen.

I cannot conclude without making a special reference to the support that the Swedish International Agency for Development has given in order that this seminar, technically assisted by the Beijer Institute whose scientists demonstrated undeniable knowledge and experience, could be a complete success.

Angola as coordinator of the regional energy sector and in the name of all the SADCC Member States expresses its appreciation to these two bodies and reaffirms its will in establishing a lasting and frank cooperation.

We believe in the future development of our relations.

To the Zimbabwe Government, delegates and to all who contributed to the success of this seminar I express, in the name of the Angolan Government, our most sincere congratulations and appreciation.

I could not possibly refrain from expressing to everybody present the most sincere wishes that 1983 be a year replenished with success.

THE STRUGGLE CONTINUES.

ENERGY DEVELOPMENT IN THE PEOPLE'S
REPUBLIC OF ANGOLA.

Energy Management.

The responsibility for energy in the People's Republic of Angola is shared by different sectors and reflects the importance which each source of energy represents in the economic context of the country and in the perspective of the country's development. However, as Angola inherited, only recently, a colonial economic structure which had no other objective than the exploitation of the riches of the territory, some reflection of this can still be felt in the organisation and development of the energy sector.

One of the most notable characteristics of colonial energy policies was an almost complete neglect of the energy problems of the rural areas, which, left to themselves, had to find their own solutions without even the minimum assistance which could have made possible a rational use of their existing resources.

Oil, which is plentiful in Angola, plays today a fundamental role both in meeting the energy needs of the country (for transport, electricity production, lighting etc,) and as the main source of income. That is why, at the level of administrative structures, the sector needs a ministry to deal with oil and gas. In 1976, a national state enterprise, SONANGOL, was established, with the monopoly of exploration, transformation and distribution of oil products.

Electricity plays an important part in the national economy, even though the country has a low consumption per capita. The special attention given to rural electrification, as well as the existing hydro-electric potential, emphasises the importance of this sector in the economy of the country. As in the case of oil, a ministry responsible for electrical energy has been established, which also attempts to coordinate all the various sectors of energy at national level, particularly with regard to the development of new and renewable sources of energy.

In 1980, a national state enterprise, the National Electricity Company was established, with the exclusive control of production, transport and distribution of electrical energy.

Firewood and charcoal, which are traditional sources of energy and of much relevance in the rural areas, are still produced and used mainly in a traditional manner. The Ministry of Agriculture is responsible for the coordination of the country's forestry resources.

Statistics on energy requirements.

Angola is a young country, which only recently gained its
independence, and which suffered a massive drain of technical and
managerial personnel which led to the collapse of the existing
weak colonial structures in the field of statistics; therefore,
it is difficult to keep up-to-date statistical information. The
situation is aggravated by the size of the country, still
devastated by wars of aggression, and by the fact that population
centres are scattered and communications difficult.

The energy sector, dependent as it is on information from other
sectors, finds it particularly difficult to gather the
statistical data so necessary for its action, as a result of the
above-mentioned problems.

The central management of the country's economy and the existence
of a national plan which covers all the various sectors of
economic activity, make it possible to make estimates and
projections on the development of the energy sector.

As far as urban centres are concerned, there are statistical data
and more or less exact estimates on the household consumption of
electricity, paraffin and butane gas. It is more difficult to
assess the situation in rural areas, especially with regard to
commercial energy.

Some attempts are already being made in this respect, and
mechanisms have been established with a view to systematically
gathering all statistical information concerning the economic and
social activities in the country, through a national body linked
to the Ministry of Planning. A very important step is the
beginning, in 1983, of a general census of population which will
provide a starting point to discover the real needs of the
country.

Sources of Statistics.

There are already, at all levels of the economic management of
the country (ministries and enterprises), planning and
statistical bodies responsible for the collection and treatment
of statistical data.

The Central Organ for Planning and Statistics, under the Ministry
of Planning, is the main source of statistics in the country,
since it has to centralise all statistical information. For each
sector, there are organs responsible for the same task.

As previously mentioned, the collection and collation of
statistical data will be considerably advanced in 1983, through
the general population census.

Sources of Commercial Energy.

The main sources of commercial energy in Angola are oil (and derived fuels), hydroelectricity and gas.

Angola has important hydroelectric resources, and hydroelectricity plays, and will play in the future, an important part in the energy context of the country. There already exist a few large hydroelectric plants which produce more than 90 per cent of the country's electricity. A few smaller plants also cater for the needs of some local populations. The main hydroelectric potential of the country is concentrated in the hydrographic basins of the Kwanza, Catumbela and Cunene Rivers, where the biggest hydroelectric plants have been built, and from which three separate systems of transport are being developed.

Thermal sources, turbines and diesel engines provide other sources of electricity, some quite powerful, which can reach thousands of units. Farms, small industries and scattered populated centres, mainly in the rural areas, have their own small systems.

The distribution of electricity is done through underground and overhead networks. These are mainly in the major urban centres, using an average voltage of 6.15 and 30kV and a low voltage of 220/380V at 50Hz.

A refinery in Luanda, with an annual potential capacity of 1.5 million tons, refines Angolan crude oil, meeting almost the entire national need for oil products used as fuels. For technical reasons, a small percentage of gas oil and butane gas is imported.

Refined products from oil are used mainly in transport, to produce electrical energy and for domestic purposes (lighting and cooking).

There have already been experiments in the use of gas to produce electrical energy. The major part of this gas was flared until the recent inauguration of a system of re-injection, which allows a more rational use of the product and increases the production capacity of crude oil.

The distribution of oil products and of gas is organised through a network of railways and roads throughout the country.

The People's Republic of Angola can be considered self-sufficient in terms of energy, not depending on any external source in any significant way.

Sources of Non-Commercial Energy.

About 50 per cent of the Angolan territory is covered by natural
forests, and the remaining part is mainly savannah and steppes
with good agricultural potential.This shows the existing
potential as far as biomass is concerned, especially of wood and
fuelwood. Some firewood is used for industrial purposes, but the
prime use is as a traditional source of energy, especially in the
rural areas. The use of other sources of non-commercial energy
for industrial or domestic purposes is not common in Angola.

Under the present circumstances, it is not possible to have a
systematic study of the consumption and requirements of
non-commercial energy. The production of firewood and charcoal
come from the consumer himself or from small producers who are
not yet organised, which makes it difficult to obtain statistical
data to confirm estimates.

Some forest plantations have begun, especially of eucalyptus,
because of its use in the railways (wood and planks for rails) as
well as in the cellulose industry.

Present Energy Projects.

In the field of electricity, important projects have been set up
in order to increase present hydroelectric production, to expand
and rehabilitate the existing plants and to create new ones. On
the Kwanza river, the expansion of the Cambambe hydroelectric
plant is planned, with some 700Mw in its final phase. The
construction of new installations is also envisaged, which will
regularise the river and increase power by about 400Mw. On the
Catumbela river, the main installation, the Lomaum plant, is also
being expanded, which should allow it, within a short time, to
have power of some 65Mw. A regulating dam will be built which
will lead to a better exploitation of the existing and future
installations. Finally, on the Matala, there will be an increase
in capacity which, in the final phase, will provide about 40Mw.

Other hydroelectric developments of lesser importance are being
drafted; some projects are already being carried out, the
objective being to meet the electricity needs of the country.
Work is already in progress. It is foreseen that in the next five
years almost 1000km of lines will be installed, with voltages of
between 60 and 220Kv.

The connection of the three main production systems is a definite
objective, but it is still under study. The electrification of
important and significant rural zones is also to be implemented
in the short term.

In the field of oil, as in the previous years, the major part of the total volume of investments will go to the research, exploration and production of oil. As in recent years, in the near future new areas will be put into exploration and/or development.

In the field of refining and petrochemicals, the Project of Study of Expansion of the Refinery and the Project of Ammonia and Urea are under study. The first one tries to match the present refinery structures to the needs of internal and external consumption. The second project will provide the embryo of a petrochemical industry, an accelerating process for the development of agriculture, and will eliminate the flaring of gas.

Energy Planning.

There is not yet in the People's Republic of Angola perfect coordination of the managment and rational use of the various energy resources. Thus, apart from the Ministries of Energy and Oil, which coordinate the main energy resources, there are other bodies which intervene in energy-related matters. This fact makes planning in the field of energy difficult. The already mentioned limitations in the field of statistics also apply to the planning process.

Planning bodies exist at all levels and efforts have been made to develop the planning process, which is considered of vital importance in the economic policy of the country.

It is compulsory to establish annual sectoral plans which are necessary to reach this objective.

Guide-lines on the Energy Policy of the People's Republic of Angola.

As the People's Republic of Angola is a potentially rich country as far as hydroelectric resources are concerned, it is clear that in the present war situation the development of this sector is remarkable. There is already a programme for the development of the production of hydroelectric energy. The use of the hydro resources, however, will have to follow a rational pattern and take into account the country's general interests.

Although the People's Republic of Angola has considerable oil resources, the use of oil as a fuel to meet the needs of the country will have to be rational, and oil will have to be used only when and where there is no cheaper alternative.

Thus, as soon as possible, small-scale electricity production, using gas oil or fuel, should be replaced by small hydroelectric plants (mini-power plants) to meet local needs. The progressive introduction of natural gas for industrial purposes is a possibility to be taken into account.

The parallel technological evolution in the field of new and renewable sources of energy must be permanent.

Rural electrification must be developed as a means of satisfying the energy needs of the population and improving its standard of living.

ENERGY DEVELOPMENT IN THE REPUBLIC OF BOTSWANA.

Introduction

Botswana is a landlocked country in the centre of the Southern African Plateau, with an area of some 582,000 km² at a mean altitude above sea level of 1,000 metres. The climate is semi-arid and the average annual rainfall is only 475mm, being both erratic and unevenly distributed. Mean temperatures vary from a maximum of 38°C in summer months to below 5°C during winter.

Apart from the Okavango area in the North and the border rivers of Chobe and Limpopo, surface water is scarce and most inland rivers are ephemeral. Because of the absence or unreliability of surface water, boreholes are an important source of supply and there are about 5,000 in operation, most of them using diesel pumps.

Arable land is scarce, and scant rainfall makes arable agriculture a precarious undertaking. Most of Botswana's land is suitable for cattle ranching and this is reflected in the fact that cattle outnumber the human population by a factor of 3.

The population, which is about 1 million (1981 census) makes Botswana one of the least densely populated countries. However, population is growing rapidly, at an annual rate in excess of 3 per cent. Population is heavily concentrated in the east where land and water resources are best, and it is predominantly rural. Although the main urban centres are growing fast they account in total for less than 20 per cent of the overall population. The larger towns are Gaborone, the capital (59,700), Lobatse (19,000), Francistown (31,000) and Selebi Phikwe (30,200). Some of the rural villages, however, have large populations, a phenomenon particular to Botswana; e.g. Serowe (23,700), Mahalapye (21,700), Molepolole (20,700).

The mineral sector accounts directly or indirectly for most of the growth of the economy. It provides about 81 per cent of export earnings (1980) and represents a 32 per cent share of GDP (1980). By comparison, the agricultural sector accounts for 11 per cent of GDP (1980) and an 8 per cent share (meat products) of export earnings (1980).

Energy resources used in Botswana reflect the economic and social structure of the country. The majority of people in the rural areas use wood for heating and candles or paraffin for lighting. It is estimated that half of the energy consumed in Botswana comes from firewood.

Other primary sources of energy include oil products and coal. Electricity, a secondary form of energy, is generated from coal and oil (diesel), and most electricity consumption is in towns and mines. Diesel is used by the railway, water-supply boreholes, and by vehicles which, although small in relative numbers, constitute the principal means of road transport upon which almost all essential services depend.

Finally, Botswana does not produce petroleum or natural gas and has no potential for hydroelectric power. National supplies of firewood are limited and are under heavy pressure around all sizeable settlements. On the other hand, Botswana has large proven coal resources, estimated at about 17 billion/tonnes, and the climate is well suited to the use of solar energy.

Energy Policies

Forty-nine per cent of all non-renewable energy used in Botswana is generated through petroleum products, and the rest through coal. The rapid rise in petroleum prices during the 1970's has made Botswana aware, as in the case of other countries, of the need to develop a concerted energy policy.

The country's rapid economic growth also means that energy consumption will grow rapidly, steps must therefore be taken to promote the use of less expensive domestic energy sources, and to safeguard essential imported supplies, given Botswana's particular geographical location. Thus, government policies in this area follow a three-pronged approach, namely:-

1. The substitution of imported oil with alternative fuels;

2. The building-up of a strategic oil reserve;

3. The development of indigenous energy sources.

A major objective of the 1976-81 National Development Plan was to substitute domestically produced coal for imported oil in the generation of electricity. In 1976, two extra 3 Megawatt coal-fired generating sets were commissioned for the Gaborone power station. This improved the position of the Botswana Power Corporation (BPC) substantially. BPC has now 15.2 MW of coal-fired plant in the Southern Division compared to 34.9 MW of maximum demand.

In addition, in order to safeguard Botswana against any instant interruption of oil imports, oil storage depots have been constructed at Gaborone and Francistown. This reserve is owned by the government and managed by commercial oil companies, which are required to maintain a continuous reserve of one month's supply.

The total capacity of the storage tanks corresponds to three months supply for the domestic economy, of which two months is in the government's account.

With regard to the development of indigenous energy sources, the objectives of the National Development Plan are spelled out as follows:-

The substitution for diesel fuel water pumping.

In this connection, two government programmes for the testing of adequate windmills began in 1979. One programme aimed at village water supplies and the other at water supplies for agriculture. There is, however, no clear indication yet that one particular design will be appropriate for widespread use. Although there will be instances in Botswana of the use of windmills, wind conditions and geological characteristics of aquifers, which are generally found at great depths, will make any large-scale implementation programme unrealistic.

The substitution of solar energy for electricity in water heating.

In this connection, a testing programme of solar heaters was carried out extensively by the Botswana Housing Corporation. The results do not yet warrant the formulation of a general policy of implementation.

The introduction of more efficient technologies for using and collecting wood.

In this connection, an experimental programme for developing and testing wood-stove designs is being conducted at the Rural Industrial Innovation Centre (RIIC).
Moreover, a project involving the assessment of renewable energy technologies (RETS) and their promotion, in particular in rural areas, is being implemented under the coordination of the Botswana Technology Centre with aid from a donor.

In summary, Government objectives for the energy sector are:-

-   To minimize dependence on imported oil, because of its unreliability of supply and rising price. This will be done by substituting domestic coal for oil in electricity generation and industrial use, and by substituting, wherever practical, wind and solar power for diesel in water pumping; and by encouraging thrift in the use of oil;

-   To safeguard essential oil supplies, by maintaining reserves and developing contingency plans to cope with any interruption to normal supplies;

- To provide electricity to meet the demands of the new mines and industries needed to fulfill the National Development Plan's major production and employment goals. This will be done by adopting a long term programme to provide flexible and abundant power supply for the late 1980s and beyond;

- To minimise the costs of electricity to industrial and private users;

- To avoid subsidising private urban electricity consumers, while retaining an element of intra-urban cross-subsidy to favour low income consumers who use electricity mainly for lighting;

- To increase the energy available to the majority of rural people by promoting the use of coal and developing strategies for the preservation of firewood sources;

- To minimise fossil energy consumption, by designing buildings that require less heating and cooling, by substituting solar energy for electricity in water heating where this is economic, and by investigating heating and cooling systems using coal for government complexes.

Institutional Framework.

Until recently the Ministry of Mineral Resources and Water Affairs had carried a de facto mandate on energy matters by virtue of it being the Ministry in charge of the Botswana Power corporation and of the Department of Electrical Engineering. The Ministry acts also as a coordinator for the SADCC energy portfolio, and monitors the implementation of the Renewable Energy Technologies programme, through the Botswana Technology Centre.

Responsibility for the Energy Mandate has now been clarified by government, and the Ministry of Mineral Resources and Water Affairs is seen as the overall coordinator of national energy matters. Regulation of the distribution of petroleum products remains the portfolio responsibility of the Ministry of Commerce and Industry.

To assume this overall coordinating responsibility effectively, the Ministry of Mineral Resources and Water Affairs is taking the following steps:-

1. Establishment of an Energy Unit as part of the Ministry's organisation;

2. Commissioning a National Energy Assessment study;

3. Development of an Energy Master Plan, which will incorporate the short and long-term objectives of the government and identify the programmes and projects needed to achieve them.

These activities are currently underway, and in fact a number of energy-related projects are being presently carried out (see details in section five).

However, the above model must be seen as a transitional one. The ultimate government organizational structure, that will reflect the mechanism which will deliver energy policies, programmes and projects, is not yet finalised. It may be, for example, that in light of the recommendations of the Energy Assessment study, there will be a need in the future to expand the Energy Unit, being developed in the Ministry of Mineral Resources and Water Affairs, into a full-fledged Department for Energy, or as an Energy Authority which is a government parastatal. One thing must be made clear, that the Government is anxious to avoid the multiplication of bureaucratic layers, unless it is strictly indispensable to do so. That means that,for at least the near future, the transitional model is seen as adequate to effectively respond to the National Energy mandate requirements.

Under this model, therefore, the Ministry of Mineral Resources and Water Affairs retains the responsibility of coordinating all National Energy matters. The establishment of an Energy Unit within the Ministry will provide the required administrative and research back-up that is needed for the formulation of policies, development of programmes and identification and assessment of projects. Furthermore, the Ministry will continue to be in charge of the Department of Electrical Engineering and the Botswana Power Corporation, to monitor activities of the Botswana Technology Centre and to coordinate energy-related programmes with other ministries, specifically the Ministry of Commerce and Industry in the area of petroleum products and the Ministry of Agriculture in the area of firewood production.

The Permanent Secretary MIRWA acts also as chairman of the Botswana Power Corporation (BPC) board. BPC is a parastatal organization and its activities are governed by the Botswana Power Corporation Act. It is accountable to Parliament through the Minister of Mineral Resources and Water Affairs. BPC supplies electricity to the main urban centres. Sales of electricity have increased from 17.9 GWH in 1972 to 420.4 GWH in 1982, reflecting the rapid industrial expansion (mainly in mining) which has occurredin Botswana. About 80 per cent of electricity sales go to mining; 6 per cent to Government institutions, including the Water Utilities Corporation (WUC),a parastatal also under the

Ministry which supplies water to urban areas; 8 per cent for domestic purposes; and 6 per cent for business and other industries. Generation of electricity is at present produced through two main stations, one in Gaborone (Southern Division) and one in Selebi-Phikwe (Shashe Division).

The Chief Electrical Engineer is the director of the Department of Electrical Engineering and is directly responsible to the Permanent Secretary MIRWA. The Department of Electrical Engineering is responsible for the procurement and maintenance of electrical installations in government buildings and institutions such as schools and hospitals. The department operates small diesel generators in rural villages which are outside the reaches of the BPC grid. The Chief Electrical Engineer is also responsible for the application of electrical regulations in Botswana and the inspection of all electrical installations.

The Botswana Technology Centre is an institution which has been created by the government to advise on new technologies, as in the fields of renewable energy, and their application, in particular, in rural areas. The centre does research in these fields but also implements programmes such as BRET (Botswana Renewable Energy Technology project), which aims to introduce energy efficiency and new technologies in rural villages. The centre is active in experimenting with windmills and photo-voltaic systems for pumping underground water. It is also involved in the design of more efficient wood stoves. Application of these technologies also necessitates extensive promotion and demonstration programmes in rural areas.

The Botswana Technology Centre is meant to operate quite independently of government bureaucracy. However, government officials representing some Ministries are represented on the Board. Furthermore, implementation of government-funded projects through the centre are closely monitored by MIRWA. The status and future of the Centre will be better defined after an appraisal mission (which should start its work shortly) has completed its report on the past activities of the Centre.

The distribution of petroleum products is regulated by the Ministry of Commerce and Industry (MCI). Since this is an area which relates to the energy sector, a de facto cooperation is established between MCI and MIRWA. Data on petroleum imports, for example, is monitored by MCI and conveyed to MIRWA for further analysis within Energy sector considerations. Under MCI, there is an institution, similar in status to the Botswana Technology Centre, which may be considered as having an indirect relationship to energy-related activities. It is the Rural Industrial Innovation Centre (RIIC) in Kanye, which, among other things, develops designs for and produces windmills and wood stoves. There is, therefore, cooperation between BTC and RIIC in the area of application of renewable energy technologies.

Lastly, activities in the Energy sector are closely linked to the national development process through the role of the Ministry of Finance and Development Planning (MFDP), which is the Central Planning agency in Botswana. A comprehensive planning process links all Ministries to MFDP, as all projects, including those coming under the Energy sector, are identified, funded and implemented in accordance with procedures set by MFDP and ultimately approved by Parliament within the National Budgetary cycle.

Energy Profile

Energy Needs.

Botswana's energy supply/demand structure is clearly dualistic. The rural population, which comprises 84 per cent of the total population, as well as many urban dwellers, depend on traditional energy, mainly fuelwood. On the other hand, the mineral-led modern sector - which forms enclaves in the few urban areas - heavily utilises conventional energy, in particular petroleum products and electric power.
Energy supply for rural areas comprises more than half the nation's total supply. But per capita energy supply for the rural population is only about one-fifth to one quarter of that for the urban population (Table 1).

Total per capita energy consumption, including fuelwood, is in the range of 900-1,000 kg oil equivalent (kg. o.e.). This level is higher than the average per capita energy consumption of the developing countries in the late 1970s. Per capita commercial energy consumption is 499 kg o.e., which is significantly higher than the average for other African countries, and very similar to the average for Asian countries.

In the rural areas of Botswana fuelwood is widely used for cooking, space heating and beer-brewing (an important source of money income),although fuelwood is becoming increasingly scarce and costly.

Other than fuelwood, a considerable amount of diesel oil is used for water pumping in rural areas. Securing water supplies from 5,000 boreholes in the country for everyday life has a vital significance for the basic human needs of rural populations. It is assumed that about 36,000 Kl of diesel oil is consumed for this activity, which accounts for one-third of diesel oil consumed in the country. The rural population also uses candles and a small amount of kerosene for lighting.

Except for small amounts of diesel oil and kerosene used in rural areas, most conventional energy is used by the mineral-led modern

TABLE 1

Energy Consumption By Urban And Rural Sector

	Traditional	Conventional	Total
Urban Sector (10^3 t.o.e.)	40-45	330	370-375
Rural Sector (10^3 t.o.e.)	420-510	35	455-545
Per Capita (kg o.e)			
Urban	290-330	2 430	2 720-2 760
Rural	560-680	50	610-730
Total	520-620	410	930-1 030

Source: UN Energy Mission Estimate, 1982

Note:
Total population in 1961 was 936 600, of which 150 000 are urban populations. To obtain the populations of 1980, annual growth rates of rural and urban populations during the period from 1971 to 1981 are used, i.e., 5.0% for total populations, 4.2% for rural area and 10.8% for urban area. Estimates of total, rural and urban population of 1980 are 890 239, 135 920, and 754 319, respectively.

sector which forms enclaves in the few urban areas. Within the modern sector, mining - especially the BCL copper-nickel complex at Selebi-Phikwe - represents a particularly heavy demand for electric power and coal. In 1980, BCL used about 130,000 tons of coal - over 30 per cent of coal produced in Botswana - directly in its concentration and smelting processes. It also used 278 GWh of electricity, which accounts for about 70 per cent of Botswana's electricity sales.

The other large energy-consuming sector is transport, which uses over one-half of total petroleum products. The growth of road transportation is the major factor which has been increasing the demand for petroleum products. The number of motor vehicles in use has been increasing since 1976 by over 10 per cent each year. In 1980, the total number of motor vehicles in use was 31,684, a 23 per cent increase from 1979. Motor gasoline consumption grew at an average rate of 9 per cent per annum during 1977-80. The demand for diesel oil - the other major fuel used by the transport sector - has been pushed up by the growth of trucks and other vehicles using this fuel (Table 2).

The manufacturing industry's energy consumption is limited. The major consumer of energy in this sector is the Botswana Meat Commission (BMC), which uses coal and electricity for meat processing.

The residential sector - defined to include houses as well as hotels, government and private office-buildings, schools, and hospitals - in 1980 consumed 2,000 tonnes of imported coal for cooking and heating, 1,300 Kl of LPG for cooking, and 77 Gwh of electricity.

Electric power generation by BPC used 228 000 tons of domestic coal in 1980, which accounts for two-thirds of the total coal production. BPC also used 2 million L of diesel oil and 5 million L of · heavy oil. Autogeneration utilised 29 million L of diesel oil. The electric power sector, including autogeneration, accounted for 23 per cent of petroleum product imports.

As for primary conventional energy supply, in 1980 just 371 000 tons of coal were domestically produced, although there are large coal resources in Botswana.

The other basic form of primary conventional energy supply is petroleum products, all imported from South Africa. The share of petroleum products in the total primary energy supply in 1980 was 40 per cent.

However, this dependency on imported petroleum products is not a direct cause of the serious balance-of-payments problem at

TABLE 2

Transport And Fuel Consumption

	Number of Motor Vehicles in Use	Motor Gasoline Consumption (Kiloliters)
1976	11 780	-
1977	20 683	35 729
1978	23 627	38 828
1979	25 789	43 112
1980	31 684	46 347
Annual Growth		
1976-80	27%	9%

Source: MEDP, Transport Statistics, Gaborone, 1980.

present. It is true that the burden of the petroleum import bill on total export earnings has increased since the world oil price increases, but the level is still in the range of 20 per cent. Considering that the average share of the oil import bill in export earnings had been about 10 per cent in 1973 and 14 per cent in 1978, the impact of oil on the balance-of-payments has not been serious.

Nevertheless, there is a possibility that an energy crisis in Botswana could occur, in the form of sudden shortages of petroleum, if there were effective oil sanctions against South Africa. To prepare for such situations, the government has already taken certain measures including the establishment of contingency plans, substitution of domestic coal for oil, and the conservation of oil for the transport sector.

Energy Resources.

Botswana has large resources of coal, which are officially estimated at 17 000 million tonnes in situ. Currently, several international energy and mineral companies are actively prospecting the coal potential for export. The government has also been proceeding on a project to expand the domestic use of coal in electric power generation, through the construction of a coal-fired station at Morupule, scheduled to start operation in 1985/86.

Hydropower potential is extremely limited, the only known potential may be on the Zambezi river.

Otherwise, Botswana has the potential of new and renewable sources of energy, including solar energy, animate power, biomass and wind.

Future Trends in Energy Consumption.

The government's most recent projection of energy forecasts makes the following assumptions:

Petroleum products for electricity would be minimised and substituted by coal;

Export of coal would begin in the late 1980's and steadily expand during the 1990's;

BPC would increase its supply of electricity to new mining projects. The ESCOM transmission line from South Africa would provide up to 31 MW of capacity to supply the Jwaneng diamond project, which starts operations in the second half of 1982. This supply is temporary and would be substituted by the Morupule power plant project in 1985/86;

Firewood supply would grow by 3-4 per cent per annum in line with the country's high population growth.

Assumptions of growth rates are shown in Table 3. Based on MIRWA's projection, it is envisaged that total conventional primary energy supply to the domestic market could grow annually by 10 per cent and 6 per cent during 1980-85 and 1985-90 respectively.

Energy Balance 1980.

Energy balances are accounting tables presenting physical flows of various types of energy from their original terms through conversion to final demand by each consuming sector. Thus, energy balances provide the basic understanding of the interrelationships between supply, conversion and consumption. Moreover, energy balances covering the past several years provide a tool to analyse change in the energy supply/demand structure in a consistent way, as well as to formulate energy supply/demand projections.

Domestic production of primary energy in 1980 comprised 1.0 - 1.2 million M^3 of fuelwood and 371 000 tons of coal. The major import of primary energy consisted of petroleum products, totalling 165 thousand Kl, equivalent to around 2 800 b/d. Botswana also imported 20 000 tons of coal for small industries and for residential use. Imports of electric power from South Africa started in the latter half of 1982, for which the primary thermal power equivalent should be indicated in the energy balance tables for 1982 onwards.

Energy conversion takes place in the coal and electric power industries. It is assumed that all the coal produced would be distributed to final consumers. However, it would be desirable also to assess the amount of coal used by the coal mine, and lost during the crushing and distribution process. The electric power sector, including autogeneration, uses 60 per cent of the domestic coal production and 20 per cent of petroleum imports. The sector also uses steam produced through BCL's smelting operation. The conversion rate for electric power is assumed to be 18 per cent.

The Energy Balance Table gives those figures in physical units and thereby enables us to identify the composition of energy supply adopted (see Table 4. 10^3 t.o.e., 10^{10} kcal, is the adopted physical unit). As shown in Table 5, traditional energy, i.e. fuelwood, plays the most important role in the nation's primary energy supply, over 50 per cent. Fuelwood's share in final energy consumption is 66 per cent, coal 14 per cent, and petroleum 15 per cent. The electric power sector's share in the final energy supply is small, only 5 per cent.

TABLE 3

Growth Assumption Of MMRWA'S Energy Supply

	1976/1981 (Actual)	1980/1985 (Forecast)	1985/1990 (Forecast)
Coal			
Production	13%	8%	37%
Supply to Domestic Market	13%	8%	7%
Petroleum Products (Imported)			
LPG	19%	17%	15%
Motor Gasoline and AV Gas	12%	12%	11%
Kerosene	10%	5%	5%
Diesel	13%	8%	8%
Fuel Oil	4%	5%	5%
Electric Power			
BPC	12%	14%	10%

Source: MMRWA, Information submitted to SADCC, July 1981, revised in June 1982.

TABLE 4

Concise 1980 Botswana Energy Balance

(Units: 10^{10} Kcal)

	Traditional	Commercial	Coal	Petroleum	Electric Power	Grand Total
Production	460-550	214.4	214.4	X	X	674.4-764.2
Imports	-	152.8	14.4	138.4	X	152.8
Exports	-	0	X	X	X	0
Total Primary Energy Supply	460-550	367.2	228.2	138.4	X	827.2-917.2
Electric Power Generation	-	-	-	-	42.2	-
Transformation and Loss	-	-125.8	-131.8	-32.5	-4.0	-125.8
Final Energy Consumption	460-550	241.3	97.0	105.9	38,4	701.3-791
Water Supply	-	18.5	X	17.7	0.8	18.5
Mining and Quarrying	-	111.8	82.6	X	29.2	111.8
Manufacturing	5.0	16.8	13.0	0.4	3.4	21.8
Transport	-	82.2	X	82.2	X	82.2
Residential/Commercial	455.545	9.5	1.4	3.1	5.0	464.5-554.5
Non-Energy Use	-	2.5	X	2.5	X	2.5

TABLE 5

Composition Of Energy Supply

	Primary Energy	Final Energy Consumption
Traditional Energy	55%	66%
Coal	28%	14%
Petroleum	17%	15%
Electric Power	-	5%
	100%	100%

TABLE 6

Composition Of Final Demand For Conventional Energy. 1980*

Water Supply	11%
Mining (mainly BCL and Botswana)	44%
Manufacturing (mainly BMC)	2%
Transport	37%
(Rail)	(2%)
(Road)	(34%)
(Air)	(1%)
Residential/Commercial	5%

Note:* Final energy demand does not include demand by energy converting sector which, in the case of Botswana, consists of charcoal and electric power generation.

Each secondary energy supply is taken to be equal to final energy demand for it. In 1980, the mining and transport sectors comprised over 80 per cent of the final commercial energy demand (Table 6). The third largest item (11 per cent) is energy for water pumping (other than in the mining sector). The manufacturing and residential/commercial sectors have a small share in final commercial energy demand, as often happens in mineral-led monocultural developing economies.

Energy Prices.

Table 7 compares various energy sources used in Botswana in February 1982. Insofar as calorific unit is concerned, prices of domestic coal and wood are evidently cheaper than imported sources of energy, e.g., imported coal, charcoal and petroleum products.

Prices of coal consumed in Botswana differ, depending upon the types of coal and the users. In September 1981, the pithead price at Morupule is understood to have been P11.22 per ton. Delivered at Selebi-Phikwe, the price was P18.79 per ton. In February 1982, Morupule coal was P20.00 per ton delivered at Gaborone. Average border prices of imported coal in 1979, 1980 and 1981 were P34.00, P44.00 and P28.00 respectively. The retail price of imported coal for residential use is typically higher, being P90.00 per ton in 1982 (or P4.50 per 50kg bag), but compares favourably with the prices of competing fuels, not only in unit calorific bases but also in usable calorific bases.

The price of fuelwood also depends on locations and the size of purchases made. The table indicates prices in Gaborone and Kanye of wood sold by donkey cart. Although prices of fuelwood have been increasing rapidly, fuelwood from woodlots cost more than twice as much as natural fuelwood. Natural fuelwood prices compare favourably with charcoal, LPG and kerosene in unit calorific bases. If wood is used with a low energy utilisation efficiency ratio, then it would become slightly less competitive than LPG in terms of usable calorific bases.

Petroleum prices are controlled by MIC on the basis of imported cost plus transportation and a marginal levy. Per litre retail prices of petroleum products in Gaborone are currently as follows:

Gasoline	0.69	p/l
Kerosene	0.52	p/l
Diesel	0.66	p/l

Different electricity tariff schedules are applied within the Northern and Southern Divisions of BPC. On average, the tariffs

TABLE 7

Price Comparison Of Energy Sources In Botswana For February 1982

Energy Sources		Calorific Value $(10^6 Kcal/t)$	Price of Unit (p/t)	Price Calorific Unit $(p/10^7 \, kcal)$	Energy Utilizat Efficien (%)
Coal (Morupule as mined wholesale)	Gaborone	5.78	20	35	12/20
Coal (imported, retail)	Gaborone	7.20	90	125	12/20
Wood	Gaborone	4.5	33	73	6/20
	Kanye	4.5	20	44	
Charcoal	Gaborone	7.0	260	371	15/20
LPG	Gaborone	10.8	820	759	70
Gasoline (normal)	Gaborone	10.5	805	767	25
Kerosene	Gaborone	10.3	606	583	45
	Maum	10.3	676	696	45
Diesel	Gaborone	10.1	582	576	30
	Maum	10.1	646	640	30
Electricity	BPC average	-	0.0509 p/kwh	591	90
Southern Division	domestic	- -	0.1217 p/kwh	1,115	50
Northern Division	domestic	-	0.0960 p/kwh	1,116	90

in the South Division are higher than those fired by oil or by coal in the North. The BPC average tariff is basically dominated by its largest consumer,· BCL, which consumed 76 per cent of BPC's electric power generation in FY 1980/81.

Energy Development Programmes

In the light of the energy policies considered above and formulated in the National Development Plan, a number of energy development programmes are underway to fulfill the objectives called for in conformity with the overall national strategies for development, which are also spelled out in the National Development Plan.

Energy Supplies: Urban and Industry

A major objective of the National Development Plan was to substitute domestically-produced coal for imported oil in the generation of electricity. The percentage of power sold generated from coal in the Southern Division of BPC rose from 28 per cent in 1974 to 71 per cent in 1980/81. Plans are underway to construct a P260 million Central Power Station in Morupule. This power station will initially contain three 30 megawatt coal-fired steam units, and this will further decrease dependence on oil. The Central Station will supply electricity to the main urban centres and to the mining industry. The present stations will remain as a back-up system. Electricity sales are expected to increase to 1,116 G.W.H. by 1990.

Energy Supplies: Rural Areas

The government is well aware that the pre-requisites for rural development are water and energy supplies. Rural villages within the proximity of the new central power station grid will be connected to the main BPC system. However, for other rural villages scattered all over the country, it will be uneconomical to do so. For these remote villages, the government is contemplating the use of smaller generators, eventually using domestically-produced coal. To this effect, the government has initiated an experimental programme for the use of producer gas plants which could be installed in certain major villages and substitute for expensive diesel generators. It will be necessary for the implementaion of this programme to develop a domestic coal marketing system in rural villages. Coal could also become a substitute for firewood in rural areas.

Renewable Energy Programmes

The government is also actively pursuing renewable-energy options. Experimental programms, such as the BRET project

(Botswana Renewable Energy Technologies), are underway to test the use of wind and solar energy sources. Windmills and photovoltaic pumps, if broadly applicable to water pumping, for example, could substantially reduce the diesel requirements of some 5,000 boreholes. In addition, the government is concerned about the rapidly depleting national firewood stock. It has commissioned a comprehensive rural energy assessment study which aims in particular to advise the government on developing and conserving firewood sources. In that context, coal will be considered as a firewood substitute, provided that its pollution diseconomies are not excessive.

Oil and Gas Exploration

Finally, the government is still interested in pursuing exploration for oil and gas in Kgalagadi, which has been identified by aeromagnetic survey as an area with potential. However, implementation of this programme necessitates negotiations with interested private companies to make ground with investigations, because it will involve huge investments.

Conclusions

Energy Planning in Botswana is not a new endeavour. Energy issues have been given due consideration for a number of years now within the central planning process. Energy objectives, policies and projects are comprehensively spelled out in the National Development Plan and implemented by clearly-identified government agencies and parastatal organizations.

Because of the prominence of energy in the international scene and the potential effects of it in a national context, it has been necessary for Botswana to give priority to the energy sector and ascertain that an adequate institutional framework does exist for the effective and efficient delivery of the energy development programmes that are required in order to meet the national development objectives.

The present framework is currently being strengthened under the overall coordinating role of the Ministry of Mineral Resources and Water Affairs. The establishment of an Energy Unit within the Ministry is expected to yield full-time coverage of energy matters and relieve the workload of the Ministry's Planning Unit, which has been carrying, together with its responsibilities in other sectors, work related to the Energy portfolio. A full-time Energy unit within the Ministry would be able to attend to the functions of Inter-Ministerial coordination, SADCC coordination, data gathering, policy research and liaison with the other relevant Ministries.

Two studies have also been initiated by the Ministry to provide supplementary elements towards the development of a general energy master-plan, as follows:

A general Energy Assessment study:

An assessment of energy requirements in the rural sector, with particular emphasis on firewood.

The results of those studies will be incorporated with the other information available on the energy sector and, together with the energy-related projects underway, will form the basis for the drafting of an updated energy master plan that will eventually become part of the National Development Plan.

ENERGY DEVELOPMENT IN LESOTHO.

National energy administration in Lesotho falls under the Ministry of Water, Energy and Mining. Apart from energy, the Ministry incorporates water and mining affairs which formerly fell under two different ministries. The creation of an energy section, in 1978, when the Ministry was formed, was in response to the energy crisis which had begun five years previously and was causing grave concern to the Government of Lesotho.

Despite recognition of the necessity for having a governmental organ dealing specifically with energy matters, the Energy Section of the Ministry still leaves a lot to be desired. The staffing position is poor. Energy matters have therefore tended to be handled on an adhoc rather than organised, systematic and regular basis. Moreover there are energy related organizations and projects, both governmental and parastatal, which operate independently of each other and without direction from the Ministry of Water, Energy and Mining. Examples are the energy section of the Ministry of Rural Development and the UNESCO funded biomass project being implemented by the National University of Lesotho.

The present deficiencies in the energy administration are due, in part, to the newness of the Ministry and it is hoped that, in time, these weaknesses will be overcome.

For the time being, however, it seems inevitable that the national energy administration should concentrate primarily on commercial sources. This is because:-

(i) Statistical data on non-commercial sources of energy is very scanty, making administration of this energy sector rather difficult to manipulate;

(ii) Empirical observation has shown that indigenous sources of non-commercial fuels are at any rate, virtually dried up, thus making it imperative to develop alternative sources of fuel;

(iii) Limited manpower and financial resources make it necessary to prioritize requirements and concentrate on areas with the greatest potential.

So far no data has been systematically collected across all sectors of the economy. However, reasonably reliable data is available in respect of commercial sources of energy such as oil, coal, paraffin, aviation gas and electricity.

Very little attention has been paid to household consumption especially in the rural areas. The only effort known to us is a study carried out by a Scandinavian organization under UNDP sponsorship some five years ago, (a copy of which is not traceable) and a research paper by March Best, of the University of Cape Town, entitled "The Scarcity of Domestic Energy: A Study in Three Villages" which, amongst other things, provided data for 'Malefiloane, a small village with some 20 families totalling 104 persons in the north eastern part of Lesotho.

The difficulties associated with estimating national demand for commercial and non-commercial energy are many and varied. For non-commercial sources one depends on data where reliability is not always beyond question. Due largely to the existence of the migratory labour system information on fuel requirements is complex.

Commercial sources can be handled with less difficulty but here too errors occur as some items of expenditure may not have been recorded. Definitional problems also arise due to overlaps in classification.

The above difficulties notwithstanding, we have made the following projections.

Commercial Sources

Electricity

Virtually all the electricity supplied by Lesotho Electricity (LEC) is imported from South Africa whose national grid is connected to that of Lesotho at Maseru (17.8MW), Ficksburg Bridge (1.5MW) and Hendrick's Drift (4.2MW). The LEC also operates a small set of diesel generators in Qacha's Nek totalling less than 1MW. In remote areas which are not connected to the national grid, institutions such as schools, government offices, hospitals and clinics generate their own electricity by diesel generators in the range of 100KW.

In 1981/82 the LEC sold 110,000 KWH of electricity. During that period the Letseng la Terai diamond mine was a major consumer accounting for about 20 per cent of electricity sales. The closure of the mine will significantly affect our projections of electricity sales for the future. Assuming a ten per cent annual increase, we anticipate the importation of 561,046,200 units of electricity will cost the LEC some M14 million in current prices. (Table 1)

To meet this projected demand substantial amounts of capital will be required by LEC to expand its electrification programme. The capital will come from internal as well as from external sources of finance.

TABLE 1

Source	Year: 1981/82 (KWH)	Year: 2000/1 (KWH)
ESCOM (RSA)	110,000,000	555,991,730
LEC + Private Diesel Generators	1,000,000	5,054,470
TOTAL	111,000,000	561,046,200

OIL

Oil exploration efforts were abandoned some five years ago and the country continues to rely on imported petroleum products and, as shown in Table 2, this dependency is likely to continue for the foreseeable future.

By and large, South African based companies are Lesotho's main source of petroleum products. Any oil sanctions against South Africa are likely to have adverse effects on Lesotho. In that event a need for an independent source of supply will have to be considered. While refining could be done in one of the SADCC member states, experience has shown that transportation of refined products could be a real problem. Assuming transit rights are granted, lack of rolling stock will be an inhibiting factor. Hence there is need for external aid to purchase rail tankers. At present 5 wagons are needed daily for fuel deliveries in Maseru, each with a carrying capacity of 36,000 litres. Actually 7 would be required were it not for the existence of a fleet of road tankers with a total capacity of 160,000 litres for transporting fuel from neighbouring South African towns into Lesotho.

In view of Lesotho's geopolitical situation, an obvious need exists for external assistance in the construction of strategic oil reserves catering for three to four months supply. Plans are afoot for the preparation of design drawings for these depots and it is hoped that assistance will be provided within the framework of SADCC at the construction stage.

COAL

A study carried out recently under UNDP assistance on the potential for coal exploration in Lesotho, has shown that there is no prospect for the occurrence of viable coal resources in this country and strongly recommends that no further efforts be made in this regard. On the basis of these findings, it appears inevitable that Lesotho will continue to depend on South Africa for coal imports for the foreseeable future.

Coal imports, over the six year period between 1975 and 1980, are shown in Table 3. Taking 1980 as a base year and assuming a 4.8 per cent average annual increase, we estimate that Lesotho's annual coal imports will rise to some 168,156 tonnes by the year 2000. The present cost of coal is M13.075 per ton, to which is added M14,00 for transport charges making a total of M27.075 per ton. This means that, in terms of current prices, Lesotho's coal imports will be in the order of some M4.5 million by the year 2000.

TABLE 2

Product	Consumption: (In million) Year: 1980/1	Annual Percentage Increase	Projected Consumption (In million litres) Year: 2000/1
Petrol	40	8	186.4
Diesel	25	14.9	402.1
Lighting Paraffin	20	3.9	39.0
Aviation Spirit	2	8	9.3
Lubricating Oils	1.4	15.6	25.4
Power Paraffin	.028	2	.42
Petroleum Gas	216,629 Kg.	Fluctuating upwards and downwards.	-
Domestic Gas	44,747 Kg.	do	-

TABLE 3

Year	Coal Imports (In Tonnes)	Annual Percentage Increase/Decrease
1975	56,000	
1976	65,000	+ 16.07
1977	56,000	- 13.08
1978	59,000	+ 5.4
1979	65,000	+ 10.17
1980	69,000	+ 6.15

WOOD

For various reasons, Lesotho retains very little of her indigenous vegetation. So devastating has been the process of deforestation that Lesotho has to import even wood for fuel. Table 4 provides figures of wood imports between the years 1975 and 1980.

TABLE 4

Wood Imports (In Tonnes).

1975	9,000
1976	16,000
1977	21,000
1978	19,000
1979	60,000
1980	33,000
1981	44,000
1982	59,000

It is estimated, on the basis of the above statistics, that Lesotho will import 240,000 tonnes of wood by the year 2000 in the absence of any effective import substitution measures. The present price of imported wood in Maseru is M19.53 per ton to which is added M14.33 for railage, giving landed cost per ton as M33.86.

HYDRO-ELECTRIC POWER

Lesotho is in an unusual situation in that it is completely devoid of fossil fuels. This situation is compounded by the fact that it is landlocked and completely surrounded by a powerful state whose policies it does not share. This state is not only exerting pressures that dominate all facets of the national economy, but is also the sole supplier of energy, whether it actually produces it (i.e. coal and electricity) or refines it and allows its transit into Lesotho (i.e. petroleum products).

This situation threatens the independence and very existence of the nation. It implies unacceptable risks in the event of an accidental or intentional breakdown in transport and delivery and creates the potential for political blackmail.

Conscious of the pressures that could be brought to bear upon Lesotho to adopt more flexible positions towards the policies of the Republic of South Africa and the unacceptable risk entailed by an interruption of supply, the Lesotho Government has attached the highest priority to the development of indigenous sources of energy.

The most obvious source of energy that could be developed in
Lesotho is hydro-power. Annually a volume of 4500 million cubic
metres of water flow out of Lesotho virtually unutilised. It has
been calculated that there is potential to generate 1250 GWH/year
which is far in excess of the projected short and medium term
requirements of the country.

Although it is technically possible to cover the entire demand
from this source, its development has been inhibited by physical
constraints that bear directly on the economics of the project.
In this connection it should be pointed out that owing to the
erratic flow pattern of the streams, (necessitating large
over-year storage) and lack of natural head, (necessitating
either high dams or tunnel transfers), the development of
Lesotho's hydro-potential requires a very high capital investment
for the installed capacity. Although the operating costs of such
plants are low, the debt servicing is such that the cost is
uncompetitive given ESCOM's present tariffs. This is the case
with most hydro-projects that have been considered so far, with
two exceptions, namely multipurpose projects such as the Lesotho
Highlands Water Project where the hydro-component is added to
what is basically a water transfer layout, and mini hydro-power
plants designed to supply isolated communities with basic power
requirements.

Generous support has been received from many donors to support
the policy of developing hydro-electric power. Table 5 outlines
the projects now being considered.

NON-COMMERCIAL SOURCES OF ENERGY

Brushwood and Dung.

The vast majority of people in Lesotho, especially those in the
low income bracket, use non-commercial sources of energy such as
fuelwood, brushwood, dung, and crop residues. In the typical
rural setting (e.g.' Malefiloane), it was estimated that the
averaged annual consumption of brushwood was 1.5 tonnes per
family. It was also estimated that the annual kraal dung
production was 670 Kg. per cow, stabled, 6 Kg per sheep or goat
and 473 Kg per horse. 98 per cent of the kraal dung originated
from cattle. The average annual household consumption of dung was
estimated at 1.35 tonnes.

The acquisition of these forms of energy is an arduous task. For
example, on average a women spends about 15 hours a week
collecting wood.

TABLE 5

Location	River	Output (Gwh/Yr)	Cost (Million M)
Lesotho Highlands	Water Project	550	1250
Jordane	Senqunyane	180	316
Letseng la Letsie	Quthing	17-80	?
Tlokoeng	Knubelu	3.5	2.07
Motete	Motete	2.5	2.45
QachasNek	Tsoelike	2.7	2.57
Mokhotlong	Bafali	1.4	1.50
Mokhotlong	Sehonghong	1.0	1.30
Sehonghong	Sehonghong	0.3	1.30
Sehlabathebe	Tsoelike	0.5	1.00
Lesobeng	Lesobeng	0.7	1.00
Semongkong	Maletsunyane	0.7	0.70
Pitseng	Tsoinyane	0.3	0.36
Ha Ntsi	Liphiring	0.08	0.20

ON-GOING ENERGY PROJECTS

Wood-lots Project.

It was precisely in recognition of the wood shortage that the
government decided to launch a woodlot project with the
assistance of AngloAmerican to ensure continuity in supply of
firewood by balancing the removal of wood by new planting.
Initially it was thought that 7000 ha. of land would be required
by 1985 yielding 7 cu. metres of wood per hectare. The plans have
been substantially revised. The project will probably go beyond
1985 and will cover 44,000 ha. catering for 240,000 families. The
problem associated with this project has been one of competition
between afforestation and other agricultural uses for prime
agricultural land. Experiments are now underway to determine the
species of trees that can grow on land which is not suitable for
other agricultural purposes.

Uranium.

A UNDP sponsored uranium exploration project is in progress but
no significant discoveries have so far been made; were such
discoveries to be made, the ore would have to be exported.

Biogas Project.

This is a UNDP Project executed by UNESCO under the auspices of
the National University of Lesotho. Its objective is to produce
biogas for cooking for a rural community. The project is still at
the embryonic stage and the results are not yet known. However,
indications are that one of the components, i.e. the Chinese
style digester, is likely to be a cost effective operation
provided the usual problems of maintenance in a village setting
are solved.

RENEWABLE ENERGY TECHNOLOGY (RET)

This is USAID sponsored project designed to test the viability of
various renewable energy technologies and where feasible
introduce them into Lesotho. Some of the technologies covered by
the project are the following:

(a) Solar Energy.

There are a few experimental solar energy installations in the
country providing hot water for domestic and institutional use.
Many are not functioning properly due to a combination of design
problems, improper installation and poor maintenance. This
technology seems to be promising provided the above problems are
overcome. The only limiting factor is that it is suitable where a
water reticulation system exists and this is not the case for the
vast majority of rural households in Lesotho. However the
government intends to support this programme wherever it is
deemed appropriate.

(b) Photovoltaic Power.

Photovoltaic power for lighting and communication is being used on an experimental basis at the Post and Telecommunication Headquarters in Maseru and many rural clinics. So far the prospects for this type of technology look good and it is intended to have the programme extended in the light of further experience.

(c) Wind Energy.

Not much is known about wind velocities and directions in Lesotho except at the proposed international airport site. However, the one obvious fact is that the state of technology does not allow for wind power to be used as a source of energy for lighting due to storage problems. Wind energy can only be converted into other forms of energy e.g. turning a windmill for water pumping purposes. There are many such wind water pumps in the country at the moment although a large number of them are not in working condition. This is mainly due to maintenance problems and, if they were effectively addressed, wind would be a viable source of energy for water pumping in Lesotho.

(d) Hydraulic Ram.

This technology (Blake ram) has been operating in Lesotho for 30 years. It pumps water from a stream into tanks for irrigation purposes. The technology is well developed and reliable. The Blake ram at the Renewable Technology Unit has been replaced by a homemade unit and it is intended to extend the programme to other locations.

(e) Thermal - Efficient Housing.

These are houses constructed to capture and retain as much solar energy as possible, e.g. by orientating doors and windows correctly, or fitting locally available materials such as discarded wool in between the walls. In this regard, it is planned to launch a campaign amongst both potential house owners and contractors in an effort to generate energy consciousness in the construction of dwelling units.

Conclusion

In this paper, we have considered the opportunities that exist in the field of energy planning and the constraints which bedevil that effort, whether administrative, technical or economic. In Lesotho, highest priority is placed on energy as it is one of the most vital aspects of the developmental efforts. The high priority placed on energy in Lesotho derives from an acute consciousness of the unique geopolitical situation and the vulnerability of the economy.

ENERGY DEVELOPMENT IN THE REPUBLIC OF MALAWI.

Energy Planning.

In order to centralize energy planning and management the Government of Malawi formed the Energy Department in 1979; its duties were:-

(a) To ensure that existing energy resources are conserved;

(b) To identify energy resources, and increase available knowledge as to the country's resource potentials and how they could be developed;

(c) To identify, and give priority to, those energy projects which are likely to produce energy most cheaply and efficiently;

(d) To control and co-ordinate energy pricing;

(e) To examine and co-ordinate such other functions related to energy as could be necessary from time to time.

In 1982, however, it became apparent that manpower requirements for the department would not be met in the short run. Hence it became necessary to utilize the already-existing institutions to discharge the above functions. To this end, an Energy Unit was established within the Economic Planning Division.

Energy Demand.

Before 1981, there had never been a systematic way of collecting energy demand data by sector. Since, as mentioned above, there was no central planning body responsible for all energy matters, the reason for the lack of such data is self-evident. However, historical data on energy demand by type of fuel does exist for commercial fuels (Table 1). With the establishment of an Energy Unit in the Economic Planning Division there will be improvements in the future. Already the Malawi Government, with the assistance of the World Bank and USAID, has completed an assessment of the potentials of different energy sources, in order to come up with major issues and options. Amongst other things, the paper stresses the need for the collection of energy demand data.

The report notes that for Malawi, fuelwood will remain a major source of energy for a very long time. Considering the rate at which this resource is being depleted, the report recommends that the government takes both short and long-term measures to avert a serious fuelwood crisis. The short term measures include the

TABLE 1

Commercial Fuel Consumption ('000 Toe)

	Petroleum	Coal	Hydro-Electricity
1970	109.1	19.5	30.5
1971	119.1	30.4	33.0
1972	129.0	35.9	39.9
1973	134.4	29.1	46.1
1974	127.1	35.3	52.4
1975	139.6	47.8	64.0
1976	143.0	41.9	67.6
1977	132.0	37.9	73.3
1978	146.1	36.4	76.4
1979	153.0	38.6	88.6
1980	148.7	31.2	96.1

improvement of the tobacco-curing processes which account for 45% of fuelwood demand. With improved efficiencies, the report observes that up to 50% fuelwood savings could be realized. The long term measures are already at the implementation stage and they include extension services to the rural population (see 5 below). However, the results in this area will take a long time to have a measurable effect. Hence government will have to put higher priority on the improvement of the tobacco-curing processes, as one means of averting fuelwood shortage.

More emphasis will also have to be put on new and renewable sources of energy. For example, mini-hydro will have to be developed alongside solar energy, as substitutes or complements to the current supply-demand mix.

There is specific attention being paid to the consumption patterns of households. This is manifested in the creation of an Energy Studies Unit in the Ministry of Forestry and Natural Resources. The function of this unit is to look into energy matters as they relate to both Urban and Rural households, including end-use technologies employed by the households. So far the unit has been doing ground work on this subject: two sets of surveys have been completed and will form the basis of the second phase of work, which is action-oriented.

The results of the first survey showed that 98% of all rural households use firewood as a source of energy to meet their basic energy demand. The survey also showed that the only commercial fuel widely used in rural areas is kerosene, which is used for lighting. The survey showed that even such alternative fuels as charcoal, crop residues, and animal waste are used sparsely, and even then only to complement the use of fuelwood.

Energy Statistics.

The National Statistics Office collects information on Commercial Energy. Such information is published in monthly statistical bulletins.

The Statistics Office is the legal authority for carrying out surveys. Any other organization wishing to conduct a survey seeks authority from the National Statistical Office. On the other hand, the NSO could be requested to collect the information and make it available to the concerned party.

Except for electricity, which is generated by a Statutory Body, the Electricity Supply Commission of Malawi (ESCOM), other sources, such as petroleum products, are supplied by private companies. However, there is always a good working relationsip with government.

Commercial Energy.

Malawi imports refined petroleum products from the Middle East.
These products come by sea either to the port of Nacala or to
Beira. Transport from Mozambique is by rail. Below is a list of
the major products:-

Liquified Petroleum Gas -   500,000 litres
Aviation gasoline   -   700,000 litres
Jet A-1   -   49,431,000 litres
Super petrol   -   54,285,000 litres
Kerosene   -   5,000,000 litres
Diesel   -   78,000,000 litres
Furnace Fuel   -   3,000,000 litres

Most of Malawi's electricity needs are satisfied by hydro-power
from the Shire river and a few isolated stations. Diesel is used
to generate electricity only in cases where a place is isolated
from the national grid. (Table 2).

Malawi imports about 50,000 tonnes of coal annually from
Mozambique, Zimbabwe and South Africa. The coal comes by rail
through Mozambique. The coal is predominantly utilized by the
industrial sector (mainly the textile and cement factories).

Non-Commercial Sources of Energy.

In the past there has been no systematic way of recording
non-commercial energy use. It was only in 1978 that, with the
assistance of IDA, a study was made on fuelwood and pole
consumption.

Fuelwood supplies about 70% of Malawi's energy needs. Around 50%
of Malawi's land area is covered by indigenous forests and
woodlands. This supplies fuelwood and poles to the rural
population, and hence is serving about 90% of the population.
There are 5 million hectares of woodland, of which 20% is
national parks and game reserves, 60% natural woodland, and 20%
forestry reserves and protected hill slopes. About 80,000
hectares are under plantation management, of these 54,000 are in
the Viphya forest reserves.

Accurate estimates of sustainable fuelwood supply are difficult
to make because of data inadequacies. In 1978, a study, carried
out to estimate the sustainable supply from various sources,
showed that it was around 8.9 million M^3. More recent estimates
show that the supply from natural woodlands on customary lands
could be as low as 1.3 million M^3. This brings the total supply
estimate to 8.0 million M^3. (Table 3).

TABLE 2

Installed Capacity

System/Source.	Capacity (MW)
Inter-connected	
Hydro	124.60
Gas turbine	15.00
Diesel	5.90
Isolated System	
Diesel	1.85
Private Generation	
Hydro	1.06
Diesel	5.25
Steam	18.23
TOTAL:	
Hydro	- 125.66
Diesel	- 13.00
Gas Turbine	- 15.00
Steam	- 18.23

TABLE 3

Fuelwood Supply

Source	Volume (100 M^3)
Indigenous Reserve	815.9
" Proposed Reserve	304.7
" Customary Land	2,406.6
Customary land clear fell	5,322.4
Reserves clear fell	57.1
District Councils	9.5
Plantation Residuals	5.4
Sawmill waste	6.2
TOTAL	8,927.8

To decrease the deficit and maintain a reasonable level of sustained yield the government has taken several steps, which include the following programmes:

1. Rural Fuelwood and Pole Project
2. National Tree-Planting Day
3. Viphya Forest Industry Trials
4. Rural Fuelwood Research Project
5. Kasungu Flue-Cured Tobacco Authority
6. National Rural Development Programme

Opportunities and Constraints.

Petroleum.

There is speculation that Malawi may possess natural gas and/or crude oil deposits at the bottom of Lake Malawi. Exploration work is continuing. However, predictions are that, even if these deposits were ascertained, exploitation would be uneconomical for several reasons, chief among them being the depth of the lake and export routes (Malawi is land locked).

Electricity.

Malawi is endowed with relatively numerous potential sites that could be developed to harness hydro-electricity. However, most of these sites are remote and very little is known about them in terms of basic engineering data. Therefore, while the potential is there, most of the development work is devoted to the Shire river, which has a well established potential of 500MW.

Since existing generating facilities are situated in one area (the middle of the Shire river) future developments will have to be diversified away from this area. A possible site is Fufu on the South Rukuru river. This site is estimated to have a potential in the order of 100MW. Owing to its remoteness, this site may have to be developed in stages. Current indications are that the development of the site may not be economical, in view of the fact that most electricity consumers are situated in the southern parts of the country, and that load factors within the vicinity of the site are too low for development of the area to be justified.

Coal.

There are five known deposits in Malawi. The most important of these is the Ngana coal field which is estimated at 7.5 million tonnes with a heat value of 22 MJ/KG, ash content of 20-30% and moisture content of 7%. Exploitation of this coal is considered to be uneconomical relative to the imported coal. The reasons for this are that the reserves are remotely located, mining costs will be too high and transportation to the major consumers, in the Southern Region, would be prohibitive. Even more important is the fact that the coal at Ngana is of low grade compared to that now imported by Malawi. In any case, more exploratory drilling work is being carried out.

Other coal deposits are in Nthalire, Lisungwi, Livingstonia and Nkhombezi areas. These are rather inaccessible and very little detailed work has been done on them. However, as the road infrastructure becomes more developed, the situation may warrant more work on these reserves to ascertain their potential.

Wind.

Wind speeds observed between 1969 and 1975 indicated average speeds in the range of 5-10 miles per hour. Such low velocities are generally regarded unsuitable for electric power generation but may suffice for shallow water pumping, depending on local conditions. Very little work is being done to harness energy from wind due to the low speeds observed.

Solar.

In Malawi the average solar intensity is estimated at $0.7KW/M^2/hr$. Despite the high level of insolation, very little work has so far been done to harness this potential source of energy. In a few hospitals, solar flat-plates have been installed to be utilized for water heating; the Department of Telecommunications is also using solar energy in a few of its remote booster stations.

Biomass.

The only constructive work done so far is in the manufacture of ethanol from sugar cane molasses. At present a plant has already been commissioned that is to produce 7 million litres of ethanol per year. The ethanol is being blended with petrol at 20% by volume. This will reduce petrol imports, hence, foreign exchange requirements. Ethanol production, however, is not a panacea for petrol problems; there are limitations; like all agricultural based industries, it is subject to the vagaries of nature. A year of bad weather, with destructive floods, persistent drought or an outbreak of disease, can destroy sugar cane, or any other feed stock, resulting in adverse economic impacts.

Apart from the ethanol from molasses very little is being done to utilize available biomas. There have been studies made on the alternative use of pinewood that was grown for use in a pulp and paper mill, but very little has come out of these studies. One alternative use of this vast supply of wood would be to produce gas that could be processed into usable petrol or alternatively the production of ammonia to manufacture fertilizer. In any case, serious work has to be done to establish an alternative use of these wood plantations.

CONCLUSION.

Malawi has so far managed to successfully contain its energy problems by identifying and acting upon the major sector issues. To ensure that the limited energy options available are to be realized within reasonable time, the government intends to keep up the momentum thus far gathered by pursuing programmes of action along the following lines:

(a) Improvement of efficiency in fuelwood use (table 4) particularly in the tobacco industry, which accounts for 40% of the fuelwood demand. The target will be to reduce the current demand of $0.13m^3$/Kg of leaf to something like $0.02m^3$/Kg.

(b) More emphasis will be placed on the promotion of efficient utilization of new and renewable sources of energy. This will be aimed at either complementing or substituting imported fuels, placing particular emphasis on the popularization of the use of solar energy for crop drying; the use of agricultural residues to substitute coal and other fuels in the industrial sector; the promotion of biogas technology.

(c) Examination of patterns of energy consumption and potential for improved efficiency of end-use technologies will also be emphasized. One emphasis will be placed on the Transport and Industrial sectors.

TABLE 4

Energy Supply Projections ('000 Toe)

	1980	1985		1990	
	Base Case	Case 1	Case 11	Case 1	Case 11
Total Demand	3,388.4	3,796	3,490	3,990	3,340

Supply by Source

Petroleum	148.7	158	137	174	152
Coal	31.2	33	42	37	49
Hydro	96.1	136	136	182	182
Ethanol	-	4	4	4	4
Tot Commercial	276.0	331	319	397	387
Fuelwood	3,029	3,382	3,088	3,510	2,870
Biomass	83.4	83	83	83	83
TOTAL SUPPLY	3,388.4	3,796	3,490	3,990	3,340

Case 1 - Increase in consumption of petroleum and reduction in coal consumption with no improvement in the use of fuelwood.

Case 11 - Decrease in petroleum and increase in coal consumption with improved efficiency in the use of fuelwood.

ENERGY DEVELOPMENT IN THE PEOPLE'S REPUBLIC
OF MOZAMBIQUE

National Energy Administration.

The national energy administration is divided into a number of different sectors. The coordination and planning of electricity supply is the responsibility of Electricidade de Mozambique (E.D.M), a state enterprise. Two major private companies exist, the Cabora Bassa Hydropower Company (H.C.B.) and the Revue Hydroelectric Society (S.H.E.R.). In addition, a number of companies possess their own generating capacity such as the sugar companies in the centre of the country. Local authorities have their own electricity plants and these are run by the municipal governments. All are coordinated by the E.D.M. as the largest state enterprise in the electrical energy sector.

The petroleum sector follows the same pattern, with PETROMOC as the largest state enterprise coordinating and planning the work of both the state and the private sector, B.P. etc., and Mocacor, which produces gas.

The State Secretariat for Coal and Hydrocarbons (S.E.C.H.) has overall responsibility for coal and oil prospecting. CARBOMOC is the state mining company and there is also a National Coal Directorate. The State Secretariat is directly under the President, whilst PETROMOC and E.D.M. form part of the Ministry of Energy and Industry.

There is no special body dealing specifically with rural energy; this responsibility is divided between a number of departments in various ministries, including forestry in the Ministry of Agriculture, the communal villages commission etc.

In the middle to late 1970's there was a National Directorate for Energy, with responsibility for coordinating long-term policy with a view to replacing energy requirements nationally from imported diesel to hydropower. This did not include the coal sector or such operations as the Railways. The National Directorate ceased to function in the early 1980's and energy policy is essentially the preserve of the various above named sectors. Overall responsibility for energy coordination and its integration with general economic development is now the responsibility of the National Planning commission. There is at present no specific body dealing solely with energy policy, although the E.D.M. has special responsibility inside Mozambique for coordinating regional energy policy within the Southern African Development Coordination Conference.

National Demand for Commercial and Non-Commercial Energy.

There is no single body devoted to collecting all the demand data to compile a national energy balance, although this was attempted in 1978. Generally, estimates of demand are collected by the relevant body in each of the respective energy sectors. There is not yet a clearly defined national framework within which these statistics are being collected. Some estimates have been made, and are being made, in relation to the ten-year plan, but this is an on-going process. Plans are of course subject to the availability of investment. Data on rural energy demand is not being systematically collected and there has been no national survey of urban and rural domestic demand. Some work has been done on specific urban locations however.

The E.D.M. has collected certain statistical information on the energy sector, outlining in broad terms the situation regarding energy consumption. Information which is meant to be supplied by industrial companies with generating capacity is not always forthcoming, or when it is supplied, it comes at irregular intervals. No detailed sectoral energy breakdown of energy consumption at present exists. PETROMOC has collected a certain amount of data and has a major share in the oil sector, with multi-national companies covering the rest. Some projections of energy consumption have been made but, again, by different sectors within the energy field.

Commercial Sources of Energy.

Hydropower Potential.

An intensive survey of Hydropower Potential for the whole of Mozambique is now being carried out. The purpose of this survey is to make an assessment of the sites where Hydropower projects can feasibly be implemented to meet energy requirements for economic development. Table 1 lists possible projects identified and installed capacities.

Of special importance is the Zambesi basin and in particular Cabora Bassa. The Zambesi is the largest river crossing the country. About 65 per cent of the estimated Hydropower resources are concentrated on the Zambesi river itself. At the Cabora Bassa Site there is a concurrence of a high potential with natural conditions, making this scheme the most feasible on the Zambesi basin. On the basis of preliminary hydrological data, the total power-production potential of Cabora Bassa has been estimated at 19,500 GWh/year (firm power).

Currently studies are being undertaken to develop a second power house on the North Bank in order to fully profit from the Cabora Bassa potential. Comparatively, the cost of firm power from alternative sources has been estimated to be as follows:

TABLE 1

ESTIMATE OF POWER POTENTIAL

Ident Number	Names of Rivers	Inst.cap. (kw)
1	Maputo	7 000
2	Umbeluzi	2 000
3	Incomati	68 000
4	Sabie	15 000
5	Elefantes	60 000
6	Limpopo	75 000
7	Save	20 000
8	Save	25 000
9	Buzi	300 000
10	Buzi	60 000
11	Lucite	180 000
12	Lucite	15 000
13	Revue	250 000
14	Pungoe	70 000
15	Pungoe	75 000
16	Pungoe	95 000
17	Pungoe	116 000
18	Messambize	1 500
19	Mese	7 500
20	Mucanha	111 000
21	Luangua ou Duangua	10 000
22	Zambeze (Cabora Bassa)	3 600 000
23	Luia	475 000
24	Zambeze (Mepanda Uncua)	1 600 000
25	Lifidzi	2 000
26	Maue	15 000
27	Mavuzi	88 000
28	Zambeze (Boroma)	400 000
29	Revugoe	1 013 100
30	Luenha	191 200
31	Zambeze (Lupata)	600 000
32	Zambeze (Downstream Lupata)	1 100 000
33	Lualua	25 000
34	Ruo	85 400
35	Muirua	15 500
36	Lugela	42 000
37	Licungo	175 000
38	Luo	22 000
39	Molocue	10 000
40	Molocue	38 500
41	Ligonha	40 000
42	Ligonha	10 000
43	Ligonha	9 000
44	Meluli	12 000
45	Meluli	25 000
46	Malema	45 000
47	Lurio	63 000
48	Lurio	120 000
49	Messalo	50 000
50	Lugenda	50 000
51	Lugenda	50 000
52	Lugenda	50 000
53	Lucheringo	20 000
54	Lucheringo	20 000
55	Luangua	5 000
56	Luaice 1	25 000
57	Luaice 2	15 000
58	Luche ou Mundoa	15 000
59	Timba	15 000
60	Messinge	45 000
	TOTAL	11 755 200

Relative terms

Cabora Bassa II	1
Mepanda Uncua (Hydro)	1.3
Nuclear	2.9
Coal	2.4

Coal Potential.

Coal has been found in several places in the central and northern parts of the country.

1. The total reserves at Moatize are estimated to be 200-250 Mm^3.

2. Another reserve, bigger than at Moatize, has been found on the northern side of Lake Cahora Bassa, at Mucanhavuzi.

3. At Minjova, east of Tete on the border with Malawi, and at Sananqua, situated between Tete and Songo, there exists a further coal deposit.

4. Two other coal deposits have been discovered north-west of Lichinga on Lake Niassa. There exist still more deposits close to the Tanzanian border.

5. Between Espungabera and Chuibabava, 150 km south of Chimoio, large deposits have also been found.

Gas and oil potential.

North and West of Vilanculos, natural gas deposits have been found with a minimum potential of 60 Billion m^3. Other deposits also exist.

Oil prospecting has been started both off-shore and on-shore.

Fuel-wood.

Large areas of the country are covered by forests, mainly in the central and northern Provinces.

Fuel-wood is used as a source of energy by one main sector, rural and urban area households, essentially for cooking. However, some industries use fuel-wood, mainly the tea factories, for drying tea.

Special attention is being given to afforestation programmes with the support of FAO, mainly concentrated on the central region of the country.

Agriculture waste.

The processing of forest products and agricultural products, such as cotton, sugar, cashew nuts and rice, produces residues of no commercial interest. The calorific value of such residues allows their use as a valuable source of energy, for electricity and steam production.

Charcoal.

No overall systematic study has been made of charcoal production but several studies have been carried out in specific locations. It is extensively used in the major urban areas.

New sources of energy.

Geothermal

Mozambique comprises 783,999 km^2. of which perhaps one-tenth lies within the East African rift system or within grabens and fracture-zones marginal to the rift. In terms of surface geology, the country can be divided into:

1. Crystalline and metamorphic terrain, mostly of Precambrian age, but including Mesozoic and Late Paleozoic bodies, forming the northern and western half of Mozambique;

2. Late Mesozoic and Cenozoic sedimentary cover, forming a thickening wedge along the east and south, and at least in part deposited over the crystalline basement.

The rift system cuts through the crystalline terrain and is either terminated against the Cenozoic cover or is buried beneath it. Earthquake seismicity and the interpretation of seismic profiles suggest the southward continuation of the rift zone beneath Cenozoic cover. Latest Tertiary and Quaternary development of the rift and graben system is indicated in Northern Mozambique by steep fault scarps, across which Quaternary sediment is juxtaposed with (largely) Precambrian crystalline rock. This is especially true in the northward extension of the rift in neighbouring Malawi.

Late Mesozoic to Early Tertiary alkaline instrusions and extrusive bodies are found principally along satellite or marginal fracture systems. Basalt and carbonatite extrusives of probable Late Tertiary age are found principally along the western boundary of the rift system. Other locations of probable Late Tertiary and/or Quaternary volcanics are (1) along faults marginal to the western rift boundary, along with the Late Mesozoic igneous bodies and (2) along the fault-controlled border between crystalline basement and Late Tertiary-Quaternary cover in northeastern Mozambique. A third possible locus of Late Tertiary-Quaternary volcanism is a graben extending south from the Tanzanian border in northeastern Mozambique.

Twenty-six thermal springs are reported in Mozambique, with the strong possibility that others exist unreported. The maximum reported temperature is 80°C for a spring NNW of Tete, located along a major fault zone in Precambrian crystalline rock. Two other springs, several hundred kilometers farther to the west on faults of this same zone, reportedly are "too hot to touch". Four springs are reported to have temperatures of 73° - 78°C, two being located along the principal rift and two being located at or near the faulted contact of Precambrian rock and Late Cesonoic cover.

The most interesting thermal area is just north of Metangula on Lake Niassa, within the rift, where vigorously boiling water was reported at the lake's edge in the years prior to the rise in water level of the lake.

Several springs of reportedly lower temperature (maximum 60°C) issue from mostly Mesozoic crystalline terrain along and west of major faults in the Espungabera-Manica areas, near the border to Zimbabwe. Locations of many of these are imprecise. Numerous other thermal springs are reported on the Zimbabwe side of the border, including a boiling spring.

A certain level of dependence on South Africa is evident within the energy sector. Both the Sonefe thermo-power plant and the railways use South African imported coal. The Cabora Bassa supply to the Maputo area goes first into South Africa where the change from D.C. to A.C. current is made. When there is no Cabora Bassa supply flowing, there is a need to import 200 GW hours per year from ESCOM.

Non-Commercial Sources of Energy.

A detailed report has recently been made on the forestry situation in Mozambique. Large areas of the country are well wooded but there are several areas experiencing a fuelwood deficit.

Current Energy Projects.

A major investment is being made in constructing new transmission lines in the centre and north of the country.

The possibility of developing Cabora Bassa II, taking advantage of the large investment already made in the construction of the dam, is also under consideration. There are clearly great possibilities here for regional energy cooperation with neighbouring SADCC member states.

Smaller-scale projects involve a hydro-power plant in Niassa Province, and construction will begin on a bio-mass generation plant in 1983.

There is keen interest in considering an integrated rural energy approach.

Studies on the oil refinery are also underway.

There are plans to open up new coal mines.

Some of the potential hydro-power sites previously identified are either in use or are being considered for implementaion. These include Elefantes, Umbeluzi, Cabora Bassa, Mavuzi, Lucheringo and in addition new sites at Moamba Major, Corumana and Massingir.

Half a dozen major consultancies have been carried out, and several companies are involved in oil prospecting.

Mozambique and International Cooperation.

Mozambique pays great attention to international cooperation with industrialized countries, international organisations and countries within the region.

As a member of the Southern African Development Coordination Conference (SADCC), Mozambique aims to promote regional energy self-sufficiency, and also the best use of the region's energy resources.

Mozambique's cooperation with the industrialized countries generally occurs in the field of training, consultancy services for feasibility studies and the supply of equipment for power development.

A special mention should be made of the Kingdom of Norway and the Kingdom of Sweden. With the support of the Kingdom of Norway, Mozambique started an ambitious programme aimed at making an assessment and overall planning of water resources and hydro-power development. Simultaneously, a construction programme of small scale hydropower schemes was started. With the support of the Kingdom of Sweden, consultancy services are being performed for the North and Central Provinces Network and for the extension of the Cabora Bassa project. Also a significant portion of equipment for power development is purchased using funds given by Norway and Sweden.

Fruitful cooperation is also established with the Netherlands,
Great Britain, Czechoslovakia, U.S.S.R., Jugoslavia, France,
Italy, Algeria, G.D.R., Bulgaria, Romania and Iraq, covering a
wide range of activities, i.e. training, the supply of equipment
for power production, technical assistance in the form of experts
working in the energy field in Mozambique, etc.. Mozambique also
has cooperation with UNDP, mainly concerning training programmes
and commodity assistance.

The Framework for Energy Planning and Development.

The objectives of Mozambican Energy Policy can be summarized as
follows:

1. To intensify the survey of existing energy resources, giving
    priority to hydropower and also to prospecting for oil, coal
    and gas;

2. To profit from the large existing hydropotential in order to
    meet energy requirements for industrial and agro-industrial
    development, by developing larger hydropower schemes and
    simultaneously erecting a National Electrical Network;

3. To develop a rural energy policy in areas far from the
    National Electrical Network, which aims to meet increasing
    energy demands and simultaneously to avoid the degradation
    and depletion of natural resources by:

    expanding afforestation programmes, together with
    explanations to the rural population about the need for
    forest conservation and its rational use;

    developing small scale hydropower projects;

    encouraging the use of windmills and watermills for
    irrigation;

    promoting solar energy for cooking and heating.

4. To optimize and rationalize the use of oil, by implementing
    the following measures:

    to improve maintenance and efficiency of equipment;

    to avoid useless oil consumption by establishing control on
    oil purchases;

    to promote coastal sea, river and railway transport;

to promote public transport and draught-animal power in the rural areas;

to control imports of equipment driven by oil, namely combustion engines;

introduction of speed limits.

5. To give permanent attention to the technology evolution of new and renewable sources of energy (geothermal, wind, waves, solar, etc.)

The National Planning Commission considers all plans and projects and has the possibility of coordinating these within the national development plan.

ENERGY DEVELOPMENT IN THE KINGDOM
OF SWAZILAND.

National Energy Administration.

There are three ministries with particular responsibility for the various energy sectors. The first of these is the Ministry of Works, Power and Communications, with the Swaziland Electricity Board and water resources coming under its auspices. Secondly, there is the Department of Geological Surveys and Mines, which forms part of the Ministry of Commerce, Industry, Mines and Tourism. In the third ministry, that of Agriculture and Cooperatives, there is the forestry section.

The three ministries concerned, concentrate their attentions primarily on commercial energy sources. At present there is no single overall energy policy coordinating administration. Coordination of economic development in general, however, is in the hands of the Department of Economic Planning and Statistics within the Prime Minister's office.

Energy Resources and Consumption.

Coal, as a non-renewable resource, and hydro-electric potential, as a renewable one, are the country's most important energy resources. Wood (firewood, woodwaste) and bagasse provide other energy resources, the latter mainly being used as a fuel for steam and power production in the sugar industry. Petroleum products account for more than 40 per cent of the total energy consumed.

A thermal coal power plant was studied in the early 1970's, but found to be non-viable in the medium term (0-10 years).

Coal.

Results of recent explorations indicated reserves of at least 200 million tonnes, although the economics of recovery are unknown at this time. Therefore, it is too early to decide upon the feasibility of exploitation.

The net production figures (in metric tonnes) for the last three years are:

1978	1979	1980
170,000	168,000	176,000

Source: Swaziland Collieries, Mpaka

The volume exported is in the range of 60 per cent, whilst the remaining percentage is consumed locally by industries and domestic households. Imports from the Republic of South Africa are approximately 20,000 tons annually.

Hydro-Electric Potential.

The hydro-electric potential of Swaziland is estimated to be around 1,000 GWH per year. At present, SEB's (Swaziland Electricity Board) total installed capacity amounts to 30.0 MW comprising two hydro-electric power stations (20.5 MW), and diesel generating plants (9.5 MW) used for supplying peak demand. Table 1 shows the power generation of Swaziland from 1977 to 1980.

Since 1973, power imports from the Republic of South Africa increased from zero to 57 per cent of total consumption.

The average growth of SEB's electricity sales is 17 per cent.

Electricity consumption by sector is:

Domestic sales	15%
Commercial sales	10%
Irrigation	25%
Power and Bulk	40%
System losses	10%

Source: SEB 1977-1980 Sales

To meet the future power demand for electricity, construction began on a hydro-electric power project in the middle of 1981, putting an expected 20 MW of additional capacity in place. This project increases installed capacity by 60 per cent, accommodates the expected growth in demand for electricity over the next three years and, at today's prices, saves the country E350,000 per month on imports of electricity.

Petroleum Products.

Swaziland has no known petroleum reserves. All petroleum products are at present imported from South Africa. The continuity of supply of these energy resources cannot be regarded as guaranteed. The energy supply situation of Swaziland could be seriously affected in the event of sanctions being imposed against the Republic of South Africa.

Table 1: Power Generation of Swaziland 1977-80 (in GWH)

	1977	1978	1979	1980
SEB Generation	123	141	115	127
Imports from ESCOM	102	85	180	200
Private Generation	N.A.	146	143	159
Total	225	372	438	486

Source: SEB Mbabane (ESCOM Electricity Supply Commission, Republic of South Africa).

The figures below indicate the volume of imports of petroleum products during the years 1977 to 1980.(Table 2)

Other Energy Resources.

Figures giving the consumption of firewood and charcoal are not available. However, Swaziland possesses great forest potential, mainly in the western part of the country where extensive commercial plantations already exist.

Approximately 280,000 tons per year of bagasse are produced by the sugar mills and, as stated before, are used for steam and power generation.

The utilization of non-conventional energy resources is being studied in the energy master plan.

As can be seen from the above, at present Swaziland is heavily dependent on South Africa for the import of electricity, coal and petroleum.

National Demand For Commercial and Non-Commercial Energy.

The recently-completed national energy masterplan has produced detailed estimates of commercial energy consumption and has provided future projections. It is a far more difficult task estimating the demand and consumption of non-commercial energy sources. There has been, as yet, no study carried out on fuelwood resources outside the commercial plantations, but there is strong evidence that fuelwood scarcity is a serious problem in certain parts of the country.

National statistical efforts rely heavily on information furnished by the private sector and cover most of the commercial energy sector adequately. The absence of a national forest inventory outside of the plantation forests means that there are no reliable statistics on non-commercial energy sources.

Current Energy Projects.

Considerable work is underway in the production of hydroelectric power using the country's considerable river resources. Future plans involve expanding the number of these projects.

An imaginative scheme concerning renewable energy resources for the rural areas is being carried out with the UNDP "Women in Development" project at Piggs Peak in the north of the country. Although on a small scale and with very limited resources, it is beginning to make an impact on the surrounding area.

Table 2:   Volume of petroleum products imported during 1977-1980
             (in '000 litres)

Product	1977	1978	1979	1980
Motor spirit	38,912.6	43,695.3	42,922.9	41,079.2
Gas Oil	40,412.5	42,387.2	45,173.1	43,702.3
Lamp Oil	4,922.9	5,554.0	5,228.9	3,969.3
Lubricating Oil	3,324.3	2,955.7	3,576.5	2,509.0
Furnace Oil	30,902.9	3,274.4	151.5	161.5
Aviation Gasoline	280.2	269.4	292.6	573.0
Aviation Turbine Fuel	424.9	857.6	2,726.9	2,378.6
White Spirit	64.2	66.0	69.9	96.3
Power Paraffin	251.6	252.1	192.4	233.6
Liquid Petroleum Gas	931.4	1,045.0	668.9	563.8
Other Products	323.6	27.1	29.6	134.7
Total	120,751.1	100,383.8	101,033.2	95,401.3

Sources: Statistical Bulletin 1980, Central Statistical Office, Mbabane.

The government is keen that the rich coal deposits in the east of the country are tapped but, at the present time, the concession-owning companies have no immediate plans to begin mining.

To reduce the dependence on imported petroleum, and hence the vulnerability of the country's economy, the establishment of an ethanol distillery project has been studied, to produce power alcohol from the molasses produced at the three sugar factories. The proposed production capacity at the final stage will be in the range of 14 million litres per year. This project is still at the preliminary stage however.

Statement of National Energy Policies.

Since a continuous and sufficient supply of energy is one of the major factors influencing social development and economic growth, and since, in the specific situation of Swaziland, there may be future constraints on the availability of primary and secondary energy (as a result of changed political situations in Southern Africa), the national energy policy has been outlined by the Government of Swaziland, through the Ministry of Commerce, Industry, Mines and Tourism.

The strategy of developing this sector is determined by the following general objective as laid out in the Third National Development Plan: 1978-79 to 1982-83.

1. To continue to expand and reinforce electricity supplies to meet the growing demand throughout the country.

2. To make the best use of Swaziland's coal and water resources for power generation.

3. To achieve independence of electricity supply as quickly as is economically feasible.

The Government of Swaziland commissioned an energy masterplan which has recently been completed. This will form the basis of the Government's future energy policy, hence some of the information contained in this paper must be regarded as being provisional.

ENERGY DEVELOPMENT IN THE UNITED REPUBLIC
OF TANZANIA.

Tanzania has significant energy resources but these received
insufficient attention prior to the 1973 energy crisis. These
resources include hydro-electricity, coal, natural gas,
geothermal energy, biomass, fuelwood and charcoal.

The objective of energy planning in Tanzania is to ensure that
its energy demands are met in the most economic and socially
acceptable manner, with an emphasis on reducing oil imports to a
supportable level. This can be achieved by expanding the
indigenous sustainable energy supplies through careful
application of an appropriate mix of proven technologies.
Achievement of this objective, however, has been and continues to
be constrained by an insufficient quality and quantity of
manpower, technologies and financial resources.

Energy Administration.

Although the Ministry of Water and Energy has overall
responsibility for energy, various aspects of energy related
issues are dealt with by several different agencies. Development
of water resources, hydrocarbons and electricity are dealt with
by the Minister of Water and Energy. Efforts to exploit coal
resources are planned, supervised and co-ordinated by the
Ministry of Minerals. Fuelwood resources are managed by the
Ministry of Natural Resources within the directorate of Forestry.
Development of village woodlots is supervised by the Prime
Minister's Office. The research and implementation of pilot
projects on new and renewable forms of energy is largely carried
out by institutions such as the University of Dar es Salaam, the
Small Scale Industrial Development Organisation (SIDO) and the
Tanzania National Scientific Research Council (UTAFITI).

The Ministries formulate policy for the exploitation of specific
energy resources under their charge. They also play a key role in
identifying the major investment options, in appraising these
options and in assigning priorities, in securing government
approval for investment, and arranging for financing. Under the
supervision and guidance of the Ministries, the Parastatals
implement the projects and programmes.

In the petroleum sector, the Tanzania Petroleum Development
Corporation (TPDC), a Parastatal wholly owned by the government,
is in charge of programmes for the exploration and development of
oil and natural gas. It also imports crude oil and arranges for
refining it into the desired proportions of products at the TIPER
Refinery, and distributes it through the five oil distribution

companies (BP, AGIP, ESSO, CALTEX and TOTAL) besides distributing directly to certain selected remote areas. Government owns 50 per cent of the shares in TIPER and 50 per cent in AGIP, while all the shares in ESSO, CALTEX and TOTAL are privately owned.

Tanzania Electric Supply Company Ltd (TANESCO), a Parastatal wholly owned by the Government, is in charge of generation, transmisson and distribution of electricity throughout the country. Presently it is also in charge of rural electrification. Rufiji Basin Development Authority (RUBADA) is a Parastatal created to plan and manage the water, land and other resources of the Rufiji river basin, and is authorised to plan, construct and operate hydro projects within the basin.

State Mining Corporation (STAMICO), a wholly government-owned parastatal organisation under the Ministry of Minerals, is in charge of the development of coal resources in the country. Research and development on new and renewable forms of energy, such as biogas, wind energy and solar energy, are also undertaken by institutions like the University of Dar es Salaam; Small Scale Industrial Development Organisation (SIDO); and Tanzania National Scientific Research Council (UTAFITI).

Sources of Energy.

There are essentially three forms of primary energy consumed in Tanzania: oil, hydro and fuelwood. In 1980 their requirements were roughly 7 per cent, 2 per cent and 91 per cent respectively. In terms of quantities, they amounted to about 760,000 tons, 170,000 tons and 9,500,000 tons of oil equivalent respectively.

Commercial Sources of Energy.

Tanzania still depends heavily on imported oil. The contribution of oil in secondary energy form was 97 per cent of total commercial energy consumption in 1960, 95 per cent in 1973 and about 90 per cent in 1980. Electricity was only 2.2 per cent of the total commercial energy consumption in 1960 but this contribution increased to 4.8 per cent in 1973, and by 1980 it was about 9 per cent. At present coal plays a very small role as an energy source, since there is only a small mine producing about 7,000 tons per annum. The increased share of electricity in the total commercial energy consumption has been attributed to a successful drive to develop hydro power sources and interconnections of major towns to the national grid.

1. Oil
Prior to 1977, crude oil and refined petroleum products were imported by the five oil companies in Tanzania. Since 1977 TPDC has been importing all crude oil requirements, while the oil

companies are allowed to import the deficit petroleum products
and lubricants. The Persian Gulf countries have been Tanzania's
traditional source of crude oil. Currently, crude oil purchase
contracts have been signed with the national oil companies of Abu
Dhabi and Quatar on an annual basis. TPDC was formerly importing
crude oil from Iran and Iraq but the purchasing contracts had to
be terminated, because of the turbulent situation in Iran and the
war between Iran and Iraq.

2. Natural Gas

Significant deposits of natural gas have been found in Tanzania.
41 billion cubic metres of gas have so far been confirmed at
Songo Songo. More recently, natural gas has been discovered at
Kimbiji (about 40 kilometers from Dar es Salaam). The Kimbiji
reserve is estimated to contain 130 billion cublic metres of gas.
These findings suggest that it is well worthwhile continuing to
appraise the hydrocarbon resources of the country. Further
exploratory work for both oil and gas, and studies for
utilization of the gas resources already discovered, are being
carried out. A decision has already been taken by the Government
to build an ammonia/urea plant using the natural gas at Songo
Songo. The plant is planned to produce 345,000 MT/year of ammonia
and 520,000 MT/year of urea, mainly for export.

3. Electricity

The present system consists of a transmission grid in the coastal
area and north-east, and a series of isolated generation and
distribution facilities each supplying power to its own limited
area.

The grid system interconnecting Dar es Salaam, Morogoro, Tanga,
Moshi and Arusha was formed in 1975, when the 220 kV line system
from Kidatu to Dar es Salaam and the 132 kV line from Hale to
Moshi were completed. In 1980 the system was further extended by
a 132 kV submarine cable connection to the Island of Zanzibar.
The grid supplies about 80 per cent of the national demand, from
hydroelectric power stations at Kidatu, Pangani falls, Hale and
Nyumba ya Mungu (NYM), and from a thermal power station in the
Dar es Salaam suburb of Ubungo. The remaining 20 per cent is
supplied by isolated diesel power stations. Most of the grid
operates at 132 kV, except that power from Kidatu is transmitted
to Dar es Salaam through Morogoro at 220 kV. The 220 kV system is
currently being extended from Kidatu through Iringa and Mufindi
to Mbeya. At present there is surplus power on the interconnected
grid which is estimated to be sufficient to meet demand on the
extended grid to the year 1987. In the meantime, areas not
reached by the grid continue to suffer power shortage, largely on
account of shortage of fuel and spare parts for the isolated
power stations. Sixteen isolated power stations are distributed
throughout Tanzania and can be geographically grouped as
follows:-

- North-West:
Comprising Dodoma, Mpwapwa, Singida, Shinyanga, Tabora,
Kigoma, Mwanza, Musoma and Bukoba.

- South-West:
Comprising Iringa, Mbeya, Tukuyu, Njombe, Tunduma,Sumbawanga
and Songea.

- South-East:
Comprising Lindi, Mtwara, Nachingwea and Mafia Island.

The isolated power stations range in installed capacity from 425
kV at Mpwapwa to 27000 kV at Mwanza, as indicated in Annex 1.
Most of the stations rely on diesel generators but there are two
small hydroelectric installations at Tosamaganga in Iringa,
1.1MW, and Moalizi in Mbeya, 380KW. The isolated stations are
separated from each other and from the grid system by distances
of 200km or more.

The total installed capacity is 372.4 MW, of which 249.2 is
hydroelectric and 123.2 is diesel capacity. The generating
capacity of the interconnected grid is 309MW, of which 247.66 is
hydro and 61.64 is thermal back-up. By mid 1983 the country's
total generating capacity will rise to 409.2 MW, by the addition
of 38.4MW of diesel power by way of additions to the existing
thermal stations and new stations.

Tanzania is fortunate in having a number of potential hydropower
resources than can satisfy the country's power requirements for
many years. The total hydroelectric potential has been estimated
to be about 3800 MW with about 19,000 GWH per year. Of this
potential, only 247 MW has been developed. The major
hydroelectric potentials are found in the Rufiji River Basis. By
far the largest single hydropower potential is at Stiegler's
Gorge on the Rufiji River, which is estimated to have a potential
of 2100MW.

4. Coal

Tanzania is fortunate in that it has major coal resources. Nine
coal fields have been identified in the southern part of the
country. The only operating coal mine in Tanzania is in Ilima
where an isolated seam in the Songwe-Kiwira Coal field is being
mined. Present production at the colliery is about 7000 tons per
year and there are plans to raise this to 20,000 tons per year.
The principal customers for the coal are local tea estates.
Detailed geological exploration and drilling has identified large
resources in Songwe-Kiwira and Mchuchuma. The estimated reserves
in each of these coal fields are about 500 million tons.

ANNEX 1

Generating Facilities-Isolated Systems.

Power Station Location	Type	No.of Units	Generating Capacity (kW)	
			Installed	Available
Bukoba	Diesel	7	1,360	1,030
Dodoma	Diesel	7	2,860	1,980
Iringa	Hydro	2	1,220	1,220
Iringa	Diesel	1	750	700
Kiabakari	Diesel	4	715	400
Kigoma	Diesel	3	765	580
Kilwa Masoko	Diesel	2	700	600
Lindi	Diesel	2	385	Nil
Mafia Island	Diesel	3	780	680
Mbeya	Hydro	2	340	270
Mbeya	Diesel	5	2,470	2,080
Mpwapwa	Diesel	4	415	345
Mtwara	Diesel	6	4,135	1,200
Musoma	Diesel	11	7,500	6,000
Mwanza	Diesel	10	27,000	15,000
Nachingwea	Diesel	4	950	400
Shinyanga	Diesel	5	1,660	1,300
Singida	Diesel	5	690	480
Songea	Diesel	4	1,235	530
Sumbawanga	Diesel	3	875	875
Tabora	Diesel	5	2,225	1,600
Tukuyu	Diesel	3	1,200	1,050
Tunduma	Diesel	3	225	225
Kondoa	Diesel	3	555	555
Babati	Diesel	3	555	555
Njombe	Diesel	3	1,500	1,500

Potential markets for coal exist in the country. Cement manufacture, tea-making, tobacco curing, brick-making, paper and pulp manufacture, and thermal power generation are among the few immediate uses of coal in the country. But heavy investment and a long lead time is required for the development of the coal mines.

Non-commercial Sources of Energy.

Fuelwood and charcoal are the two major types of non-commercial energy used in the country. Tanzania mainland has a total land area of 883,343 km^2 with about 50 per cent of the land under forest cover. In aggregate, the country is expected to have enough basic forest goods and services; however, in localised areas there is an acute shortage of basic forest goods. The natural forests which supply fuelwood and charcoal to the fast growing population are the savanna and intermediate woodlands. These forests have low annual volume increments which are estimated to range between 1 - 2m^3 solid round wood per hectare per annum.

The potential supply of fuelwood and charcoal from the existing natural forests in 1981 was estimated to be about 19 million m^3, while the total consumption was estimated to be 34 million m^3. There is a wide gap between potential supply and demand, consequently leading to deforestation, which is extending rapidly outwards from densely-populated residential areas.

Being a renewable energy resource which can be produced within the country, it is envisaged that fuelwood will continue to be the main source of domestic energy in Tanzania for several years. However, acute shortage of fuelwood and charcoal are inevitable due to the high intensity of clearing of natural forests going on. Fuelwood scarcity is being experienced in many regions of Tanzania, which, if allowed to continue, will render more serious socio-economic problems, mainly soil degradation accompanied by a reduction in agricultural production, which could lead to food shortages for the rapidly increasing population. Efforts are to be made to plant more trees throughout the country as an integral part of sound socio-economic development. Contribution by other forms of non-commercial energy such as solar, wind, biogas, etc are negligible at present. But research and development work is already being undertaken to increase the use of such renewable forms of energy. Solar energy is used in certain parts of the country, for crop drying. Wind energy is used for pumping water in villages.

Estimating National Demand For Energy.

Attempts are being made to prepare a national energy balance. But lack of data on supply and demand of the various forms of energy make it difficult to prepare the energy balance.

The high cost of oil imports and foreign exchange constraints have led the government to introduce conservation measures, such as rationing of petroleum products, pricing and a Sunday driving ban. Restriction on the importation of motor vehicles has limited the consumption of gasoline. Because of the austerity measures being taken, the actual consumption of petroleum products does not reflect the true demand for the products in the country. In 1978, a French consultancy firm, BEICIP, attempted to carry out a market survey as a basis for a feasibility study on the TIPER refinery expansion. TPDC update the study from time to time. Annex 2 shows how petroleum products consumption has evolved during the years between 1975 and 1981. Considering that oil prices will rise in the long term and conservation measures are still in force, an attempt has been made to forecast the demand up to the year 1990, keeping in mind the economic problems the country is facing. These estimates are shown at Annex 3.

Information is available on sales of different petroleum products but information on the end-use of each product is not readily available. An attempt to estimate the consumption of each product by sector is presented in Annex 4.

The demand progress of the electrical system in the country was carried out two years ago by M/s Acres International of Canada, through an extensive analysis of industrial and non-industrial consumption over a period of 35 years i.e. up to the year 2015. The short term forecast (1980 - 1985) was developed from an analysis of historical energy sales, the national industrial strategy and by consideration of forthcoming energy-consuming projects. Beyond 1985, the forecast was extrapolated to the year 2015 using growth relationships based on an analysis of historical demand and the expected long-term economic growth. The system growth rate was expected to be 9.8 per cent annually up to the year 1985, and thereafter 5.5 per cent per annum to the year 2015.

In order to determine the realistic and optional generation development, in the light of the present economic situation, a review of the load forecast was recently conducted by TANESCO by re-assessing the status of specific on-going industries and envisaged development up to 1985, in terms of output, financing, design and construction progress, and raw materials input. The results reveal that electrical energy growth rate is expected to be 8 per cent per annum for the ten year period beginning in 1981.

The principal source of fuel for over 90 per cent of Tanzania's population is wood. In the rural areas, it is mainly used as firewood and in the urban areas it is used as charcoal. About 95 per cent of the country's wood consumption is for fuel. In the

ANNEX 2

Consumption Pattern-Petroleum Products, Tanzania 1975-1981 (In Metric Tons)

Product	1975	1976	1977	1978	1979	1980	1981	Average increase (decrease) in consumption.
LPG	5,544	6,590	5,805	5,690	5,762	5,790	5,853	1.3%
MSP	52,446	58,623	56,410	61,317	71,737	70,921	64,176	3.8%
MSR	52,500	52,838	46,438	44,440	45,146	42,748	47,037	(1.6%)
IK	68,565	75,355	73,639	96,805	75,224	77,485	79,252	3.7%
Jet A-1	23,996	29,574	22,714	28,045	44,457	55,800	44,096	14.4%
G.O.	205,059	236,579	215,612	217,968	229,555	259,322	242,567	3.2%
LDO	56,214	57,686	54,406	52,999	41,766	56,585	53,988	0.7%
F.O	143,823	167,784	169,969	115,094	131,583	115,539	122,275	(1.1%)
AvoGas	5,224	3,209	2,611	3,284	2,352	2,078	1,613	(15.6%)

Source: TPDC, DSM

ANNEX 3

Estimates Of Petroleum Consumption-Tanzania 1982-1990 (In M.T.)

Product	1982	1983	1984	1985	1986	1987	1988	1989	1990
LPG	5,929	6,006	6,084	6,163	6,243	6,324	6,406	6,489	6,573
MSP	66,640	69,199	71,856	74,615	77,480	80,455	83,544	86,752	90,083
MSR	46,294	45,563	44,843	44,134	43,437	42,751	42,076	41,411	40,757
IK	82,168	85,192	88,327	91,577	94,947	98,441	102,064	105,820	109,714
JET A - 1	50,428	57,669	65,950	75,420	86,250	98,325	112,091	127,784	145,674
G.O	250,426	258,540	266,917	275,565	283,832	292,347	301,117	310,151	319,456
L.D.O	54,463	55,592	56,766	57,989	59,262	60,587	61,968	63,407	64,906
F.O.	123,464	172,475	191,057	190,935	190,482	190,034	189,590	189,152	188,717
Av.Gas	1,371	1,179	1,038	1,000	1,000	1,000	1,000	1,000	1,000

Source: TPDC, DSM

ANNEX 4

Petroleum Products Consumption By End-Use Sector-1981 (Metric Tonnes)

PRODUCT	AV GAS	JET A -	LPG	MSP	MSR	IK	GO	IDO	FO	LUBES & GREASES	SPECIALTIES	TOTAL	
Air Transport	1,613	49,720	-	-	-	-	-	-	-	361	44	51,738	(7.6%)
Road Transport	-	-	-	64,700	47,034	398	155,029	-	-	1,027	6	268,194	(39.2%)
Rail Transport	-	-	-	-	-	119	28,149	29	15,994	705	16	45,012	(6.6%)
Water Transport (Ex.Bunkers)	-	-	-	3	3	5	1,858	1,857	-	211	-	3,937	(0.6%)
Agriculture	-	-	-	-	-	-	22,702	8,467	-	2,261	2	33,432	(4.9%)
Construction	-	-	-	-	-	-	17,321	379	52	405	135	18,292	(2.7%)
Industries	-	-	1,392	-	-	4,880	14,196	27,583	94,627	2,519	77	145,274	(21.2%)
Household/Domestic	-	-	4,462	-	-	70,088	-	-	-	-	-	74,550	(10.0%)
Mining	-	-	-	-	-	-	1,912	-	-	-	-	1,925	(0.3%)
Commercial	-	-	-	-	-	-	-	-	-	11,901	1,009	12,910	(1.9%)
Power Generator	-	-	-	-	-	-	1,400	15,667	11,602	290	-	28,959	(4.2%)
TOTAL	1,613	49,720	5,854	64,703	47,037	75,490	242,567	53,982	122,275	19,693	1,289	684,223	(100%)

next two decades no substantial change in this dependence on fuel
is envisaged. At present, some kerosene is used for cooking, but
rising prices are scarcely likely to restrict any major increase
in the use of this fuel. Electricity and coal may also be used
for cooking to a limited extent.

Fuelwood in most cases is collected free from nearby forests by
villagers and, as such, very little record is kept on consumption
levels. However, available estimates by the Ministry of Natural
Resources indicate that per capita average annual consumption of
fuelwood for domestic purposes is about 2.0m^3. The consumption
varies significantly from region to region, ranging from 0.7m^3 in
Dodoma, and 0.9m^3 in Mwanza and Shinyanga to 2.6m^3 in the Tanga
and Mbeya Regions. The variation is mainly due to availability of
fuelwood, cooking habits and climatic conditions.

Fuelwood is also used for tobacco curing, tea drying and fish
smoking. It is estimated that 50-60m^3 of fuelwood is being used
annually for brick burning. However, the fuelwood consumption for
brick burning is increasing mainly in those areas near to forest
resources. Limestone burning, ceramics and pottery consume on
average annually about 270,000m^3 of fuelwood.

Estimates of national demand for the above energy forms are very
difficult to make, particularly those relating to fuelwood,
largely on account of the limited quantity and quality of
necessary resources. The need to estimate energy demand for
Tanzania is, however, becoming increasingly realised by technical
planners and the government, and it is envisaged that the present
estimates will be improved upon as the national resources base,
including manpower, technology and funds, improves with time.

Current Energy Projects.

Petroleum Projects.
As regards petroleum exploration, the government has recently
given licences to Shell, IEDC (Internaional Energy Development
Corporation) and Agip-Amoco to prospect for oil and gas in
different parts of the country. TPDC's discovery of natural gas
at Songo Songo and Kimbiji has prompted government efforts to
seek external financial assistance for drilling of additional
wells at Songo Songo and Kimbiji. Petro-Canada and the Opec Fund
have pledged to provide financial assistance to the drilling
programme.

Several studies aimed at identifying projects for government
consideration have been, or are currently being, undertaken.
These studies include:

1.Alternative uses of natural gas, such as power generation, production of methanol, both for export and conversion to gasoline, and as a direct source of energy, especially in the cement industries to replace fuel oil.

2.Refinery Expansion. This project envisages the installation of a 1 million-tonne per year atmospheric distillation unit to bring the refining capacity to about 1.6 million tons of light crude oil per year. Studies on the project have been completed but government has postponed implementation of the project because of the adverse economic situation prevailing in the country, as well as uncertainty about obtaining a reliable crude oil supply source.

3.Blending Ethanol with Gasolines: Studies on this project have been completed and the project is to be implemented by the National Chemical Industries Corporation. A similar study is currently being undertaken by AMBONI group to produce ethanol from sisal waste. The 'gasohol' will be consumed locally.

4. Studies for the construction of three strategic storage depots at Tanga, Mwanza and Makambako to provide capacity for 60 days petroleum products requirements for the neighbouring regions. However, because of financial constraints, this project has not taken off.

Electric Power Projects.
Mtera Hydropower Project.
Mtera Hydropower Plant is the only hydropower station that can be developed and commissioned so as to be fully operational by 1987, and thus avoid an envisaged power shortage from that year. The project involves the construction of a power house with an installed capacity of 80MW, intake and tail race tunnel.

Stiegler's Gorge Project.
This is a multi-purpose project with the objectives of hydropower generation, food control, irrigated agriculture, fisheries, tourism etc. The project would comprise a concrete arch dam 134m. high, to form an ultimate reservoir of 1300 km^2 with an installed generating capacity of 2100 MW, and will be implemented in four phases. The first phase will involve construction of the main dam and a power station of 400 MW installed capacity. In the second phase, a power station of 800 MV installed capacity will be constructed. A series of saddle dams will be constructed in the third phase, to enable the two power stations to generate their full capacity. The fourth and last phase, which may involve construction of a 900 MW power station, will need to be studied in greater detail prior to implementation. Assuming the access road and bridge will be completed by 1985, Phase 1 of the project could be commissioned by 1982, if funds could be raised by mid 1983, so that construction may begin in 1985.

Hydropower projects in Kagera Basin and Mara Region.
A feasibility study for the Kagera Basin Project - Rusumo Falls
(80MW), is being done under the joint Kagera Basin Organization
of Rwanda, Burundi, Uganda and Tanzania; completion will take
some time. Detailed investigations of Kishanda valley (200MW) and
Kakono (400MW) will be carried out at an appropriate date in the
future. In the meantime, mini hydro sites are to be identified to
provide power to the Kagera Region. It is expected that a
comprehensive feasibility study for the Mara River Power
Development will be carried out when funds become available.
These projects, when completed, will feed into the expanded
National Power Grid.

Rufiji Basin Master plan for hydropower development.
RUBADA, assisted by NORCONSULT of Norway, is in the process of
preparing a master plan for the Rufiji River basin. This involves
considering all possible sites which are already identified, as
well as new sites to be identified. Once this plan is completed
in mid-1983, then a feasibility study will be undertaken for the
preferred site.

North-west Extension.
The North-west Extension of the Grid is planned to connect Iringa
- Dodoma - Singida - Shinyanga - Mwanza on a 220kV radial line,
Shinyanga - Tabora and 132kV line extension from Mwanza to
Musoma. The plan is to complete the work in stages, from 1983 to
1985. Interest has been indicated by several donor countries, and
negotiations for tying up the financing have begun.

Kidatu - Morogoro 220kV Second Circuit.
In the existing grid, there is only one 220kV line connecting the
main hydro staion at Kidatu to the rest of the grid, including
the main load centre of Dar es Salaam. Any outage or disturbances
on the line affects the entire sytem. In the feasibility studies
for the Kidatu project, a second circuit is recommended.
Furthermore, recent stability studies do establish the need for a
second line. Another point of serious concern has been
maintenance, which is almost impossible, due to the fact that part
of this line passes through very difficult terrain in the Mikumi
National Park and this makes access very difficult.

In view of the above, it is proposed to provide a second circuit,
of a 220kV line between Kidatu and Morogoro, and route it along
the road from Kidatu to Mikumi village and then along the
national highway to Morogoro.

South-east Extension.
The South-east regions of Mtwara and Lindi, presently fed from
diesel stations, are beset with chronic problems of lack of
spares, uncertainty of fuel supply etc. The load demand at both

Mtwara and Lindi is growing fast as a number of industries, including a textile mill at Mtwara, are planned for implementation in the next few years. Accordingly, a comprehensive load forecast of these areas has been carried out which shows that demand will grow to 16MW by 1987. The economic analysis concerning a continuation of thermal generation and a 132kV transmission line option, shows that the 132kV transmission line is the optimal solution, It is, therefore, proposed to proceed with the extension of the transmission line from Dar es Salaam to Lindi and Mtwara, with a spur-line from Lindi to Masasi, so as to interconnect the towns of Newala and Nachingwea through 33kV lines.

Grid Control Centre.
With the new transmisson extensions and the proposed generation schemes, system operation and control will become complex, and will require a grid control centre to coordinate generation, transmission and distribution of power, so as to obtain minimum energy supply costs and optimum system efficiency.

Mini hydro Project.
Feasibility studies are being undertaken at different identified locations with the assistance of Sweden, Norway and Finland.

Implementation of the projects will be started as soon as the studies are completed and funds made available.

Songwe - Kiwira Coal Project.
Plans have already been made by the State Mining Corporation to establish a coal mine at Songwe - Kiwira, to produce 150,000 tons of coal per annum. An agreement has already been signed with the Chinese authorities for assistance in the development of the mine. The project is expected to start this year and be completed by 1985.

Projects on New and Renewable Energy.
Installation of biogas plants is being done at various parts of the country, by the Small Industries Development Organization of Tanzania. So far, 45 plants have been erected and 9 plants are to be constructed this year. Windmill installation for water pumping is undertaken by regional authorities, where it is found to be suitable. Research projects on various forms of new and renewable energy are being carried out by the University of Dar-es-Salaam and the National Scientific Research Council.

FuelWood Project (Afforestation Programme).
Since 1975, intensive afforestation efforts have been undertaken for fuelwood production. An encouraging upward trend in hectares of land planted each year has been experienced, as outlined below:-

Year	Hectares of trees planted
1975	3,280
1976	3,678
1977	5,776
1978	7,161
1979	7,946
1980	9,490
1981	12,050

In spite of the encouraging trend, the current planting targets need to be increased to 20,000 hectares/annum, accompanied by more efficient use of fuelwood, and encouragement of natural forests, in order to meet effectively the fuelwood demand, as well as to maintain a sound vegetation cover.

Most of the projects mentioned above have been conceived with a view to catering for national energy demand. The grid extension and Stieglers Gorge power projects, however, bear great potential as SADCC regional projects in terms of facilitating international links.

Energy Planning and Development.

Energy planning is recognised in Tanzania to have become an important issue in developing a comprehensive and integrated energy policy. Neither planning nor policy-making can be done in isolation from overall development strategies. We have to admit that even though the planning for the electrical sector was well attended to, based on a number of studies, planning of the other energy forms has been less co-ordinated. It is strongly felt that there is a need for developing a framework within which the programmes for all energy sub-sectors are integrated. As a first step towards this, attempts are being made to form a national energy balance.

Electric Power Sector.
The principal planning objective in the power sector is the provision of adequate electric energy at least cost. This is achievable if generation planning is based on maximizing indigenous resources and interconnecting currently isolated load centres to the grid.

Strategy.
The development strategy must clearly recognize the following basic facts:

1. A careful selection of energy resources to determine the priority and sequence of development, keeping in view among other things:

The lead time necessary for the development of various generation schemes from conception to full operation;

The capital investment requirements of each generation scheme, as well as total annual costs;

The possible impact of the project on the environment;

2. A power strategy parallel to the Government's deliberate decentralization of the industrial base is necessary, to provide the requisite amounts of power to the industries being established throughout the country.

3. In the agricultural sector, the current five-year plan envisages the development of extensive irrigation schemes throughout the country, including the establishment of agro-mechanised systems and re-inforcement of agro-related industries.

4. The possibility of developing the mineral sector will also have a direct influence both on power and demand generation resources development.

5. There is an evident potential to export power to neighbouring countries which are not so fortunate with respect to their indigenous resources, and which may wish to purchase hydropower from Tanzania.

6. The present railway system of the country is run entirely on diesel powered engines. In view of the overall oil situation, consideration could be given to electrifying the railway system to make use of the indigenous resources available.

Guidelines:
In consideration of the above factors, the following guidelines are important:-

1. The highest priority is being given to hydroelectric development, inclusive of mini and microhydro plants.

2. Phasing out of diesel plants systematically and connecting isolated towns on high voltage transmission lines, by extension of the coastal grid to form a National Power Grid.

3. Coal is an indigenous source and should, where feasible, be developed to provide additional generation capacity and to improve supply reliability under drought conditions.

Petroleum Sector.
As mentioned earlier, demand management measures have been taken
to limit consumption of petroleum products to supportable levels.
The amount of products the nation can afford to buy is
distributed on a priority basis, with first priority being given
to the directly productive sectors, such as agriculture and
industry.

In the important field of oil exploration, it is realized that
the search for oil is very risky, expensive and requires
sophisticated technology. Like many oil-exploring nations,
Tanzania cannot afford to go it alone! A cocktail of our own and
foreign resources, featuring exploration areas, funds and
technical skills, is needed and genuine efforts made to build
local skills in negotiating favourable exploration agreements and
in carrying out oil exploration work.

Following the completion of a nation-wide airborne geophysical
survey, compilation of up-to-date seismic data and the
establishment of a comprehensive and modern legal frame-work,
namely, the Petroleum (Exploration and Production) Act 1980,
various international companies have expressed an interest and
have acquired exploration rights in the country. Two carefully
negotiated production sharing agreements were signed with SHELL
International and the International Energy Development
Corporation in September and November 1981 respectively, and an
on-going exploration agreement with AGIP and AMOCO was extended.
Interest has also been shown by important foreign donors
including NORAD, the World Bank, the OPEC Special Fund and Petro
Canada, who have provided or pledged invaluable financial and
technical assistance to oil exploration work in Tanzania.

Conclusion.

The hydro-electric, coal, natural gas, geothermal, biomass and
fuelwood energy resources and projects discussed above constitute
significant and essential opportunities for energy development in
Tanzania. In addition, the country has people eager to be trained
in various technical and administrative fields, political
stability and sound development polices. Despite these
opportunities, however, energy development in Tanzania is
difficult, and in some cases slow, due to numerous constraints.
These constraints include, insufficient and unreliable data for
energy planning, a low level of technical skills, lack of
financial resources, the long lead-times and high risks involved
in energy investments. Tanzanians believe they can ease
difficulties in energy development through cooperative or
joint-venture endeavours with other willing and able nations and
international institutions. In this regard, the SADCC countries
and their international cooperating partners constitute a golden
opportunity in furthering Tanzania's energy planning and
development.

ENERGY DEVELOPMENT IN THE REPUBLIC OF ZAMBIA

The Nature of the National Energy Administration.

Several bodies deal with energy administration in Zambia. The most important ones are:-

1. The Ministry of Power, Transport and Communications (MPTC). In this Ministry there is also:

    (i) a Power Wing (Headquarters) and a Department of Energy;

    (ii) a Secretariat for the National Energy Council (NEC);

2. The Ministry of Mines which is responsible for surveys, through the Geological Department, for new sources of hydrocarbons.

The Government of the Republic of Zambia has taken measures to streamline the energy sector and rationalise its execution by all the interested wings of the Government.

The Republic of Zambia, while paying great attention to commercial sources and forms of energy, is also conscious of the importance of non-commercial sources of energy. In both cases, the introduction of these sources of energy will not be made haphazardly, as this could be disastrous. The Government is approaching this whole area of man's endeavours as an integrated and planned exercise.

Data Collection

Demand data is, to a large extent, systematically collected, but there is room for improvement in data collection and collation.

Household consumption in rural areas is mainly based on firewood, and some figures for this consumption exist. These figures have been used for the Zambian Energy overview which has been elaborated for the SADCC Energy seminar. However, these figures are not reliable enough to be used as a basis for forecasting demand, although this is part of the planning procedure. The significance of this form of energy will be established following the completion of a wood consumption survey project which starts in January, 1984, under UNDP financial assistance.

Projections for coal demand, electrical generation and petroleum products exist.

Statistical Sources

The 1980 census is the main source of information for population-correlated statistical data.

The other source is the present knowledge of consumption of electricity, coal and oil products. The total of this consumption information must be considered quite reliable. However, the data cannot be considered quite as reliable when they are broken down into sub-sectors. For example, it seems quite unlikely that agriculture should only account for 1.14 per cent of the total petroleum products. It is more likely that this figure covers the direct sales of petroleum products to farmers while the consumption by farmers who buy the products at filling stations may be accounted for and lumped together under "Transportation". Similarly, the consumption of farms owned by commercial and industrial firms may be accounted for under "Commercial and Industrial".

The following must be considered the major sources of information on energy:-

1. Zambia Electricity Supply Corporation Ltd.(ZESCO);

2. Zambia National Energy Ltd.(ZNEL);

3. Maamba Collieries; and

4. The Oil Companies.

Commercial Sources of Energy

The commercial sources of energy are:-

1. Charcoal.

2. Electricity.

3. Oil Products and Coal.

Only crude oil is imported by sea upto, and then through, the TAZAMA Pipeline from Dar-es-Salaam to the Indeni Refinery in Ndola. Earlier, Zambia received all of its supplies of oil products from South Africa and Zimbabwe. The construction of the TAZAMA Pipeline and the Indeni Refinery in Ndola were a direct result of political developments in Southern Africa. These sources no longer play a role in the supply of oil products to Zambia. However, it is never a favourable position for a country to be dependent on only one supply route for such an essential commodity as oil, because of the risk of technical breakdowns. It is hoped, therefore, that the cooperation within SADCC will open other new and reliable supply sources.

Non-Commercial Sources of Energy

No systematic attempt to record the supply of non-commercial energy has yet been made. However, as firewood plays a role as an energy source, especially for cooking, in rural areas, it is felt that such a reliable record is necessary in order to implement a proper energy plan on this form of energy. It has not yet been decided whether this should be achieved through studies to be undertaken by ourselves or whether this should await the UNDP study mentioned under item 2.

Energy Projects

The following energy projects are now in progress in Zambia:

1. Possibilities of using slurries from the Maamba Collieries as Domestic Fuel, making Briquettes;

2. Improvement of charcoal production, using steel kilns instead of traditional kilns;

3. Biogas production in rural areas using manure;

4. Solar energy for air heating (drying purposes).

The Framework for Energy Planning and Development

Planning and Initiatives

Energy Planning in developing countries is hard work - harder than in developed countries - because developed countries often have a lot of basic information, not only about demographic and economic conditions but also about the energy situation, and information not at hand can often be easily gathered. However, the hard work should not keep developing countries away from planning. On the contrary, proper planning in a field like energy, which takes away so high a percentage of hard-earned foreign exchange, is even more necessary for developing countries than for developed ones. But a plan must aim at something, and the energy plan for Zambia, now in the process of being started up, has the following three main aims:-

1. Reduction of oil dependency;

2. Electrification of rural areas;

3. Reduction of the consumption of firewood and charcoal.

The country-wide energy plan will be based on the coordinated energy plans for each of our 9 Provinces.

The Planning Procedure will run through the following steps:-

Step i - Preparation of the Planning Procedure.
Preparation of the procedure to be adopted in the collection and collation of information on Provincial and District Authorities, Industrial Corporations and Companies, Transport Companies and the Public about the future planning procedure, elaboration of questionnaires and the execution of step ii, below, in one district to gather experience.

Step ii - Collection of Data.
The purpose of this step is to find out how much energy is used at present, which kind of energy for which purposes (in industry, agriculture, transport, household etc.), from which sources, and in which part of the country (down to the District level).
The cooperation of provincial and district authorities, industrial corporations and companies, transport companies etc, will be sought to formulate a detailed analysis of this information for policy formulation.

Step iii - Elaboration of Future Trends for Energy Consumption.
The purpose of this step is to make estimates for the future energy demands. These estimates must be based upon the findings under step ii above, upon the expectations of developments in the different sectors of society (industry, agriculture, transport, household etc.) and upon the expectations of future prices for the different types of energy.

Step iv - Proposals With Regard to Future Energy Supply.
The purpose of this step is to make proposals on what changes should be made in energy supply, bearing in mind the main aims of the plan. The possibilities of changing from one energy source to another and the possibilities of using new and renewable energy sources will be assessed. The proposals will deal with short, medium and long term possibilities. The costs involved in accomplishing them will be calculated with regard to employment, industrial development, forestry, foreign trade, then will be assessed and evaluated.

A schedule with regard to the time necessary to implement the proposals will be made, taking into account the financing required for their execution.

Step v - Political Decisions and Implementation of the Results of
Step i.
During this procedure, possible changes of existing laws and
necessary new laws must be considered in order to have a proper
legal basis for the implementation of the plan.

Time Schedule

If the necessary staff are available, the steps of the energy
plan can be accomplished according to this time schedule:

Step i	approximately	...	4 months
Step ii	approximately	...	6 months
Step iii	approximately	...	6 months
Step iv	approximately	...	6 months
Step v	Proposals will be given during step iii		

Initiatives.

Planning often means that no initiatives are taken during the
planning process. There is normally no reason for this if the
initiatives are selected in such a way that they can support the
planning procedure. In Zambia we have selected 9 such
initiatives, some of these are already underway:-

- Possibilities of building mini and small hydropower stations
  in rural areas (in progress);

- Possibilities of changing the existing diesel-generated power
  plants to hydropower or coal or electricity, changing of
  production methods, insulation, use of waste heat or waste
  products;

- Oil saving in transportation, by electrification of railways,
  improvement of public transportation, urging the use of
  cheaper fuel (e.g. diesel or LPG) in private cars or
  long-running petrol cars (e.g. more than 12 Kilometres per
  litre of petrol);

- Biogas production in rural areas (in progress);

- Ethanol production from molasses (in progress);

Staff and Organization.

The future work described above will require a considerable
strengthening of the staff of the Department of Energy.

In doing this, there are two possible approaches:-

1. A large department could be built up with a staff able to do
    almost everything by itself. This is the approach some
    countries have chosen, having established Ministries of
    Energy with staff ranging from 100 to 300 people.

2. The other way to go about it is to build up a Department of
    Energy with fewer people - between 25 and 30 - over some
    years. Their responsibilities would be to initiate,
    coordinate and participate in the work mentioned above and to
    put the results into force. A very considerable amount of
    work must be done by people in the local authorities, in
    corporations and companies and by consultants.

It is felt that only a few expatriates should be employed in the
Department of Energy, as it is considered more advantageous to
Zambia to Zambianise the Department as fast as possible, which,
however, implies that considerable amounts should be allocated in
the annual budget for studying abroad and for participation in
international workshops, conferences and meetings.

ENERGY DEVELOPMENT IN THE REPUBLIC OF ZIMBABWE

Energy is critical to all aspects of national development, and as such its management and development should be given the greatest attention by government. The developing, non-oil producing countries, like Zimbabwe, find themselves in competition with industrialised countries for available oil, and the price of that competition is high. The energy problems of such countries are serious and urgent, and vigorous and visionary policies will be needed to solve these energy problems. The energy policy must have as its main objective the guarantee of energy supply to the industries and peoples of Zimbabwe at a price which reflects the full resources cost and the long term availability of the various energy sources.

Zimbabwe, emerging from the war of liberation and embarking on massive programmes of reconstruction, and a new thrust in economic development, faces a herculean task in its attempt to achieve self-sufficiency in energy. Energy requirements are indeed necessary for the realization of the many economic programmes the government intends carrying out.
Indeed, the energy demands for Zimbabwe will continue to rise for many decades to come.

The high price of imported fuels, the problems of security of supply for petroleum fuels, and the continued depletion of this non-renewable energy source compel Zimbabwe to look more and more to the development of its indigenous energy resources, both conventional and non-conventional. While this direction in energy development should eventually lead to a guarantee in energy supply, and will save the country greatly in foreign exchange, the initial costs for embarking on new energy projects will not be light. The demands on the available financial resources of Zimbabwe which are needed for the many other social and economic programmes will perforce be heavy. These are the challenges Zimbabwe must face.

On the other hand Zimbabwe does have abundant indigenous energy resources, which, if developed intelligently and utilized rationally and judiciously, could meet the energy requirements of the country for many generations to come. We need to tap all our available energy resources, for no one energy source provides a panacea.

What, then, are these energy resources which Zimbabwe must develop?

Coal

Zimbabwe has an estimated 30,000 million tonnes of coal, mostly in the north west Zambezi Valley; and the south east Sabi-Limpopo Valley. The true figure is probably higher. These coal resources are of different types and qualities, and must be exploited to the maximum benefit of the country. Coal in Zimbabwe is used in the iron and steel industry, in the ferrochrome industry, and for export. As a direct energy source it is used in power generation, for heating purposes and in transport. We must continue to develop our coal reserves to meet the above mentioned applications.

However, consideration must also be given to other applications of coal not currently being undertaken in Zimbabwe. I speak here of the production of synthetic fuels and chemicals from coal.

At the moment coal is mined only at Wankie, where about 3 million tonnes are produced annually. Production of coal will necessarily rise, with the construction of new thermal power plants, and with more diverse applications of coal being introduced. Consideration must therefore be given to the possibility of opening other coalfields. But before this is done, Zimbabwe must carry out a comprehensive study of all its coal reserves so as to determine which coal is best for what applications.

Power

Zimbabwe gets its electricity supplies from Kariba Dam, and thermal power stations scattered across the country. More sites for the construction of hydroelectric schemes are available on the Zambezi River, and their exploitation must be carried out without delay. The exploitation of small scale hydroelectric schemes for regional use will also be encouraged.

Coal will play an important role in power generation, especially since hydroelectric sites are limited. The existing thermal power stations are nearing the end of their lifetime and new stations should be commissioned to augment the capacities of the hydroelectric power stations, being mindful that coal is a wasting asset which has many other important applications.

Transport Fuels

The importation of transport fuels demands an inordinate share of the country's foreign exchange, and presently petroleum fuel is the major energy problem facing Zimbabwe. However, developments to reduce imported fuels are well underway. Use of ethanol as a transport fuel was introduced in Zimbabwe in mid 1980, and presently spark-ignition engines are being run on a 15 per cent ethanol - 85 per cent petrol blend. The possibility of increasing the ethanol/petrol ratio is being studied. The ethanol used in the blend fuel is produced from sugar cane grown at the Triangle Estate in the south east of Zimbabwe. Consideration is being given to the establishment of more sugar plantations for ethanol production to meet increased fuel demands for the future. The conflict between land use for fuel production and food is under debate, and must be resolved to the best interests of Zimbabwe and its peoples. Studies on the possibility of using other substrates - such as corn, cassava and sorghum - for ethanol production are underway.

Work on diesel extenders has lagged behind that of petrol blends, but even in this area many possibilities are being pursued. In particular, work on the use of vegetable oils as diesel extenders has been going on for sometime, and generally the results are encouraging. Possibilities of blending diesel with alcohols and petrol are under investigation.

The production of synthetic fuels from coal is a matter to which Zimbabwe must give great attention. As the oil reserves dwindle, coal-derived fuels and chemical products will move in to fill the gap. Possible coal-derived fuels and chemical products are synthetic oil, synthetic gas, ammonia, plastics, resins, methanol and many others. The use of these products in Zimbabwe, and possibly for export to our neighbouring countries, merits consideration. Ammonia, with its use in the fertilizer industry, and in the manufacture of explosives is an attractive product, since Zimbabwe presently imports large quantities of ammonia. The production of synthetic fuels from coal, and the establishment of a coal-based chemical industry are important issues which government is seriously studying. For Zimbabwe the studies must first cover comprehensive physical and chemical analyses of our coals, and a review of the coal technologies to identify conversion processes most suited to our coals; and the products we desire.

Woodfuel

The problem of the availability of wood is a serious energy issue in Zimbabwe - for over 5 million people in the rural and urban areas rely on this energy source for their cooking and heating needs.
It has been a neglected energy source in the past, but government has declared that it shall not be so anymore. The problem of meeting the energy requirements of rural people is being tackled in a multipronged way:

1. Re-afforestation and afforestation, to ensure continued supplies.

2. Efficient use of woodfuel, by introducing cheap wood stoves, to extend the use of available supplies.

3. Woodfuel substitutes.

4. Strict conservation methods.

Other Alternative Sources of Energy

Attention is being given to other energy sources not mentioned above, to determine their possible contribution to the energy requirements of Zimbabwe. Applications of solar energy for water heating, cooking and crop drying will be pursued. Zimbabwe has a high insolation, and the use of this renewable energy source must be extensively considered. The use of biogas plants, utilizing animal and agricultural wastes will be actively encouraged. It is possible that these plants could provide the heating, cooking and lighting requirements for many of our people, especially those in the rural areas. Other alternative sources of energy whose use will be encouraged in Zimbabwe are wind energy and bagasse.

Conservation

Energy conservation is regarded as an energy resource. Judicious energy management and its use must be encouraged. Both large industrial concerns and individuals must be made conscious of this fact. Wastage of energy must be avoided, and more efficient utilization of energy encouraged. Where regulations become necessary to enforce conservation, they shall be introduced.

These, then, are the broad areas along which Zimbabwe intends to move to meet its energy requirements, and coal will play a crucial role in Zimbabwe's quest for self-sufficiency in energy. We have embarked on a comprehensive survey of the energy requirements and consumption patterns of the country, to identify those issues on which a broad national energy policy and plan will be based. The government is encouraging a more vigorous approach in research and development into our indigenous energy resources. The government is committed to developing a technological base and the generation of skilled manpower for undertaking the projects on energy development.

The government is determined to provide the finance and capital for the projects already underway and for those being contemplated, and we have no doubt we shall succeed.